TRACING YOUR
BLACK COUNTRY
ANCESTORS

FAMILY HISTORY FROM PEN & SWORD

Birth, Marriage and Death Records
David Annal and Audrey Collins

Tracing Your Channel Islands Ancestors
Marie-Louise Backhurst

Tracing Your Yorkshire Ancestors
Rachel Bellerby

The Great War Handbook
Geoff Bridger

Tracing Your Royal Marine Ancestors
Richard Brooks and Matthew Little

Your Rural Ancestors
Jonathan Brown

Tracing Your Pauper Ancestors
Robert Burlison

Tracing Your Huguenot Ancestors
Kathy Chater

Tracing Your East End Ancestors
Jane Cox

Tracing Your Labour Movement Ancestors
Mark Crail

Tracing Your Ancestors
Simon Fowler

Tracing Your Army Ancestors
Simon Fowler

A Guide to Military History on the Internet
Simon Fowler

Tracing Your Northern Ancestors
Keith Gregson

Your Irish Ancestors
Ian Maxwell

Tracing Your Northern Irish Ancestors
Ian Maxwell

Tracing Your Scottish Ancestors
Ian Maxwell

Tracing Your London Ancestors
Jonathan Oates

Tracing Family History on the Internet
Christopher Patton

Tracing Your Prisoner of War Ancestors:
The First World War
Sarah Paterson

Tracing Your Tank Ancestors
Janice Tait and David Fletcher

Great War Lives
Paul Reed

Tracing Your Air Force Ancestors
Phil Tomaselli

Tracing Your Second World War Ancestors
Phil Tomaselli

Tracing Your Secret Service Ancestors
Phil Tomaselli

Tracing Your Criminal Ancestors
Stephen Wade

Tracing Your Legal Ancestors
Stephen Wade

Tracing Your Police Ancestors
Stephen Wade

Tracing Your Jewish Ancestors
Rosemary Wenzerul

Fishing and Fishermen
Martin Wilcox

Tracing Your Canal Ancestors
Sue Wilkes

TRACING YOUR BLACK COUNTRY ANCESTORS

A Guide for Family Historians

Michael Pearson

Pen & Sword
FAMILY HISTORY

First published in Great Britain in 2012 by
PEN & SWORD FAMILY HISTORY
An imprint of
Pen & Sword Books Ltd
47 Church Street
Barnsley
South Yorkshire
S70 2AS

ISBN 978-1-84415-913-0

Typeset by Concept, Huddersfield, West Yorkshire.
Printed and bound in England by CPI Group (UK) Ltd, Croydon, CR0 4YY.

Pen & Sword Books Ltd incorporates the imprints of
Pen & Sword Aviation, Pen & Sword Family History, Pen & Sword Maritime,
Pen & Sword Military, Pen & Sword Discovery, Wharncliffe Local History,
Wharncliffe True Crime, Wharncliffe Transport, Pen & Sword Select,
Pen & Sword Military Classics, Leo Cooper, The Praetorian Press,
Remember When, Seaforth Publishing and Frontline Publishing.

For a complete list of Pen & Sword titles please contact
PEN & SWORD BOOKS LIMITED
47 Church Street, Barnsley, South Yorkshire, S70 2AS, England
E-mail: enquiries@pen-and-sword.co.uk
Website: www.pen-and-sword.co.uk

CONTENTS

PREFACE

The challenge of writing a local history book with family history advice was one I approached with some trepidation. I am not an expert in either subject, but have knowledge of both. My task was made more difficult because of the wealth of information available to me, and what to leave out often became a more difficult decision than what to include. I hope this book gives a taste of the breadth and depth of the Black Country, and how to research ancestors who lived there.

When I became interested in genealogy the Internet was still in its infancy; it was almost anarchic, not dominated by corporates vying to sell goods and services. This meant that any information discovered on the Internet had to be treated with caution. Over time corporate sites have emerged and many 'amateur' sites have matured; in many cases you can view original documents on screen, in exactly the same manner you would look at a document in a library or archive. A number of commercial sites are mentioned in the book because no single site can service all requirements. A word of warning, however, you could spend a lot of money subscribing to sites, so before you commit yourself it may be prudent to see if there are free sites that hold the information you need. It may also be worthwhile weighing up whether to visit the local archive, many of which have free access to online resources that you would have to pay for at home.

During the writing of this book my collection of local history material has swollen markedly. I have delved around looking for books, pamphlets and maps to recommend. I have also suggested using some modern guides and books on specific subjects, which will be useful if an ancestor is thought to have engaged in a particular profession or perhaps been an inmate in a workhouse. Amazon and eBay have been essential in enhancing my collection of reference material, enabling me to purchase out of print books very cheaply, often as good as new. It is also worth considering subscribing to one of the family history magazines that are available in newsagents. Genealogy is constantly changing, with new collections being made available and new technology being developed.

Software to record family trees is evolving and widening its base to include iPads, iPhones and other similar devices, allowing you to take your family tree with you on research trips.

There is also a wealth of Black Country books and other material such as CD-ROMs available, and more are being released all the time; you will be spoilt for choice. Many of the antiquarian books I have quoted may only be found in libraries and archives, but they are well worth seeking out for their contemporary points of view.

If you are new to the Black Country or genealogy, welcome, you have arrived at an exciting time and I hope you enjoy your hobby and all the information it brings. You may be tempted simply to compile a family tree, with the specific intention of going back as far as you can. I hope this book encourages you to stray off the track leading to William the Conqueror and try some of the other highways and byways that will provide you with more challenges and a much richer picture of your ancestors. You may have stories of skeletons in the closet, a scandalous anecdote or a tale of great wealth, but try and keep your feet on the ground and work methodically. If you find a jewel in the crown then that is absolutely fantastic and I encourage you to write about it and develop the story as far as you can; if you don't have such a jewel, this doesn't make your research any less interesting or exciting.

Enjoy your hobby and enjoy this book. I hope you will get hours of entertainment and fulfilment from it and the research you will be able to carry out after reading it.

Michael Pearson
May 2012

ACKNOWLEDGEMENTS

T here are a number of people who have helped me with the writing of this book, but first I must mention my wife Linda. As with all my projects, she has endured hours of me typing or reading, totally absorbed in what I am doing; I cannot multitask and am almost deaf and blind to the outside world when concentrating. We have had some interesting trips around the Black Country as a bonus of my work, and we have visited as many of the museums and facilities as possible to provide you with as much information as possible. I would like to thank Stan Hill, former editor of the *Blackcountryman* magazine who has an absolute wealth of knowledge and material on the Black Country. I am also grateful to the Black Country Living Museum for allowing me unfettered access to photograph buildings, vehicles and exhibits in the search for material for inclusion.

Pen and Sword have also been very supportive. I would like to thank Simon Fowler, my managing editor, for his feedback and suggestions. Simon has many years of experience working at The National Archives, and this shows in the advice and guidance he has given me. Rupert Harding, my commissioning editor, also deserves a mention. His patience has been critical, especially when I took on a role at work that meant I had to put the book on hold for over three years. I hope everyone who has been involved in the production of this book is as pleased as I am with the result.

INTRODUCTION

The Black Country

This book seeks to give you an insight into the region of the Midlands known as the Black Country. This opening chapter explores how the region acquired its name, its boundaries and its origins, as well as the on-going debate as to which communities are included in it and which are not. The importance of the Black Country during the Industrial Revolution is described in chapters 1, 2 and 3, while chapter 4 looks at transport. Dialect is covered in chapter 5, along with other subjects such as living conditions and institutions like hospitals, asylums and work-houses. There is a wealth of archives, museums, societies and places of interest you can use to assist your research, and full details can be found throughout the book, and in particular in chapter 9. Chapter 6 gives an insight into what your ancestors did when not at work. Chapter 7 examines the religious history of the region, while crime, punishment and the police are examined in chapter 8. The appendices assist with tracing military ancestors and understanding how local government structures developed through the ages.

Boundaries of the Black Country

The 'Black Country' is not a county, it doesn't have officially defined borders, nor does it have an administrative structure to look after its interests; this makes the region singularly different. County boundaries are well defined, as are other regional boundaries – the Lake District, for example. It is only recently that the Ordnance Survey has included the 'Black Country' name on its local maps, after a long and vociferous campaign. The original border was based on geology; it was the 30ft (9.15m) thick coal-seam that lay beneath the region and formed a defining feature. This was Britain's thickest and richest seam of coal which, together with adjacent seams of thin coal, iron, limestone and clay, supported the development of the industry. The coal lay beneath Wednesbury, Darlaston, Wednesfield, Bilston, Coseley, Tipton, Dudley, Brierley Hill and Halesowen, together with nearby smaller townships, and at greater depth beneath West Bromwich, Oldbury and Smethwick. This seam led to the transformation of a rural backwater into one of the largest and most important industrial areas in the world. It has often been described as 'the workshop of the world', and its output helped to create and maintain the British Empire.

It was not only the presence of minerals such as coal and iron that turned the Black Country into the industrial region it became. The geology was important, as the size and shape of the coal-seam defined the borders. Also important was the geography of the region; the Black Country's position in the centre of England meant it had an advantage, although it had no direct access to the sea. There is no major river through the region, but the Stour and Tame are part of the Black Country's story because they provided transport links and power for watermills. Transport links had to be developed to serve the emerging industry. Examination of early maps shows a distinct difference between the development of towns and villages between the north and south of the region. The area roughly north of Dudley seems to be more heavily populated, even in the late seventeenth century, with a greater concentration of villages and towns than in the south. There was a better network of roads in place connecting the settlements. In contrast, the south had only two settlements of any significance – Dudley and Stourbridge – and consequently the road network there was less developed. Canals had not yet been built in the region, but when they were they largely followed industry. A comprehensive series of waterways was constructed in a relatively short period of time (the development of roads, canals and railways is dealt with in chapter 4).

Rapid industrial growth led to the region being described as 'black by day and red by night'. From the early 1700s scores of industrial townships and villages emerged, and from the late nineteenth century many local councils were created. In 1974 all the townships within the Black Country were consolidated into the four Metropolitan Boroughs of Dudley, Sandwell, Walsall and Wolverhampton. The boundaries of the metropolitan borough councils form a wider interpretation of the area covered by the Black Country than purely the definition based on the 30ft coal-seam. The geological definition would probably satisfy the purist, but ask many residents of the four metropolitan boroughs where they live and their response would be 'The Black Country', rather than the administrative area of the West Midlands.

It is important, for the purposes of this book, to define the area to be covered. For that reason I have chosen to use the local authority areas of

A map of the Black Country, showing the main towns, 1830. (Atlas of English Counties, 1830)

3

Dudley, Sandwell, Walsall and Wolverhampton. There may be occasions when I mention areas slightly outside these boundaries, for example, the archives at Stafford and Worcester have material that may assist those undertaking research into the area. Before 1974 the Black Country was part of three counties: Staffordshire, Worcestershire and Warwickshire. A useful resource of old maps from 1579 to the 1870s is Eric Richardson's *The Black Country as Seen through Antique Maps*, which has recently been re-printed by the Black Country Society.

The Black Country Name

A good place to start is the name, something that sets this region apart from anywhere else in the country. Probably one of the most often asked questions at the Black Country Society is when and why the Black Country received its name. The obvious reason is linked to the industrial reputation and descriptions of the area during the nineteenth and twentieth centuries. There is no evidence to support any other origin for the name. The more taxing question concerns when the Black Country received its name. This has long been the subject of much debate and reference to historical material to find out the answer.

Mining, of both coal and ironstone, was carried out as early as the late thirteenth century. By about 1600 blast furnaces existed, although during this period the region was still very rural. During the English Civil War, for example, Bilston is recorded as having a population of 500, in 1780 it was about 3,000 and the town was largely agricultural. By 1821 the population had risen to 12,000, with many newcomers, mainly from Shropshire and Wales, attracted by the high wages being paid in local iron works.

In 1830 William Cobbett, author of *Rural Rides*, went on his 'Midland Tour' and he wrote of the iniquities of the 'truck' or 'tommy' system in what he called 'the iron country'. The *Oxford English Dictionary* quotes a book written by JC Young, published in 1834, as the earliest reference to the words, but the phrase 'the black country' was not capitalised. The dictionary also mentions an article in the *Daily Telegraph* of 12 December 1864 that contains the phrase: 'By night the Black Country blazes up lurid and red with fires', so it is clear that by this time the title was in wider use.

Some think the name originated in 1836 in a book by William Hawkes Smith, *Birmingham and South Staffordshire or Illustrations of the History, Geology and Industrial Operations of the Mining District*. However, the name is not found here, although it comes close, with the coalfield shown black on maps and reference made to 'black compartment', 'sable tinted province' and 'dusky space'.

The earliest written record is in *Lloyd's Weekly London Newspaper*, dated 12 April 1846. This contains a report on a postponed quarterly meeting of the ironmasters. The meeting was called to fix iron prices in the region, after a drop in price was forecast as a result of falling demand for iron. The report states: 'Trade, in fact, is almost paralysed by the delay and uncertainty that attend them [Robert Peel's free-trade measures]; there will be a season of great distress and feverishness all over the "black country".' It is worth noting the use of lower case in 'black country', which perhaps implies the name is not yet widely used in the rest of the country.

Another early recorded use of the name is in William Ford Vance's *Sermons – With a Voice from Mines and Factories* (1853). It is thought that from about 1815 geological maps used black tint to define coal measures. Vance was Vicar of Coseley in the early nineteenth century.

By 1860 the phrase is accepted and well known, for example, in Walter White's *All Round the Wrekin* (2nd edn, 1860). The first book title to feature it was probably *Walks in the Black Country and its Green Borderland* (1868) by Elihu Burritt, for many years the American consular agent in Birmingham. His definition of the area is novel: a 20-mile radius around Birmingham Town Hall, though he later distinguishes Birmingham from the Black Country proper. Burritt graphically describes the view he and a colleague enjoyed one evening, from the top of the walls of Dudley Castle:

A writer of a military turn of fancy might say that it was the sublimest battle-scene ever enacted on earth ... There was an embattled amphitheatre of twenty miles span ridged to the purple clouds. Planted at artillery intervals on this encircling ridge, and at musket-shot spaces in the dark valley between, a thousand batteries, mounted with huge ordnance, white at the mouth with the fury of the bombardment, were pouring their cross-fires of shot and shell into the cloud-works of the lower heavens. Wolverhampton, on the extreme left, stood by her black mortars which shot their red volleys into the night. Coseley and Bilston and Wednesbury replied bomb for bomb, and set the clouds on fire above with their lighted matches. Dudley, Oldbury, Albion, and Smethwick, on the right, plied their heavy breachers at the iron-works on the other side; while West Bromwich and distant Walsall showed that their men were standing as bravely to their guns, and that their guns were charged to the

Dudley Castle courtyard, showing the ruined walls. (Author's collection)

muzzle with the grape and canister of the mine. The canals twisting and crossing through the field of battle, showed by patches in the light like bleeding veins.

Burritt paints a wonderful picture of the industrial landscape from the highest vantage point at the centre of the Black Country. White makes many references to the phrase, and it seems likely that the use of 'Black Country' was an accepted description of the area, for example:

Then taking a trip by rail to Dudley we see the chemical corner of the Black Country, as it may be called, for it is so much overspread by chemical works that you look as vainly for beauty as at Bilston. As seen from the station, Deepfields appears to be afflicted by rest-less streams as well as smoke, besides sharing in disagreeable smells that float free as the wind. After all this, how refreshing to the eye are the slopes at the foot of the Wren's Nest.

I think the first thing for me, having been born and bred in Dudley and lived all my life in the heart of the Black Country, is the real emphasis on local identity. Ask anyone where they come from and you are more likely to hear 'Dudley, Cradley, Netherton' and so on. This is often accompanied by 'in the Black Country'. Compare this response to that of someone from, say, Birmingham. Their first response is likely to be 'Birmingham', not 'Acocks Green, Erdington, Kings Heath' etc.; the city comes first, followed by the area. A visitor today might think we live in a large suburban area, and may miss the significance of the village names. This is not the case for those born and bred here; they still see themselves as coming from their village.

Beginnings of the Black Country

The Black Country was only black for a limited period of history. At the time of the Norman Conquest the area was rural, sparsely populated and offered little to the economy. This remained the case throughout the medieval period, mainly because trade was largely carried out via rivers and there is no significant waterway running through the region. Also, because the Romans did not see fit to build a road here, there was nothing to generate an increase in trade. This early period will be examined in more detail in chapter 5, when dialect is discussed. Wolverhampton is one of the oldest towns (now a city) in the area. It dates from about 984, and had a market charter granted in 1258. Dudley is mentioned in the Domesday Book, as is 'Hala', which became 'Hales' in 1177 when Henry II granted it to David ap Owen, Prince of Wales, hence the modern name 'Hales Owen'.

Catalysts for the Black Country becoming a major centre for industrial expansion were the South Staffordshire thick coal-seam together with ironstone and plentiful limestone. Another factor was the work of Dud Dudley, a pioneer in smelting iron using coal, and the decision of John Wilkinson to build a mineral blast furnace in 1766 at Bradley. The region also developed a comprehensive canal network as a result of the demand for better transport. Early industrial development was based around Birmingham, Walsall and Wolverhampton, which were seen as emerging manufacturing centres. The central plateau between these three towns was seen as an area to supply the centres with coal and other minerals to enable the manufacture of goods.

A number of key families were instrumental in ensuring the growth and success of Black Country industry. Among these was the Dudley family, and the Earls were major developers and employers in the area, the Round Oak Iron and Steel Works being only one example of their achievements. Another influential family was the Foleys, which started to become well known with Richard in the late sixteenth and early seventeenth centuries. Benjamin Mander was born in 1752, when the population of the market town of Wolverhampton was only 8,000. He

The Saxon preaching cross, the oldest relic in Wolverhampton. Located in the grounds of St Peter's Church, the ancient collegiate and parish church, it dates from about AD 994. (Author's photograph)

started his japan-tin business in the town; japanning is the process of coating sheet metal with a hard jet-black lacquer. The business grew and developed in Wolverhampton, and the Manders eventually became a major name in paint and varnish. The site of the Mander Paint Factory is now occupied by the Mander Shopping Centre, which stands in the heart of Wolverhampton. In later generations members of many of the founding families became politicians.

As the coal field was worked further, the Black Country border extended, with development starting later and industry continuing slightly longer around the fringes. There are as many opinions on the boundaries of the Black Country, and who is 'in' and 'out', as there are people. I have already alluded to communities wanting to belong or believing they belong, especially around the edges, and there is much local rivalry concerning this.

Any industrial area relies heavily on its workforce, and this was equally true of the Black Country. Mining communities tend to become close-knit, as was the case in the Black Country region. Industrial development increased steadily, and enabled the population to manage the need for workers; there was immigration, but immigrants integrated quickly into the region, which always felt relatively local. One reason for this is explored in the discussion of dialect in chapter 5. Another factor was that the wealth generated by industry meant people did not leave the region to work elsewhere. There were a few examples of emigration, for example, the departure of local miners to Nanaimo on Vancouver Island in Canada, and in more modern times the population has, of course, become more mobile. The demise of heavy industry on the scale it existed during the early twentieth century, combined with work elsewhere and greater ease of transport, has meant the edges of the region have become somewhat blurred. There are now more towns and villages outside the boundary of the South Staffordshire coal-seam that are associated with the Black Country.

While the resources and position of the region were important, and Black Country men and women enabled the region to industrialise, ultimately it was the industrialists and philanthropists who recognised the significance of the region. The Earls of Dudley, for example, owned many of the mines around Dudley; one Earl also built the Guest Hospital for his workers. John Corbett, the 'Salt King', who built Chateau Impney in Droitwich, also established a hospital, the Corbett, in Stourbridge. People like Job Garrett, James Brindley, the Mander family, John Newcomen, Matthew Boulton and an almost endless list all contributed to the development of the region.

Why is the Black Country Special?

What makes the Black Country different? There is a real emphasis on local identity, a multitude of 'characters' and a desire to be recognised as a region in its own right. The rapid growth and then decline of industries that made the region, followed by modernisation with new industries and greater reliance on service industries has maintained the region's position on the map. This includes the canal network, neglected for so long, but now rejuvenated for the growing leisure market; this will be examined in greater detail later on in the book.

Geology has also helped shape the emergence of the Black Country. Without the minerals that lay beneath the ground there would have been no Black Country, and the area would probably have remained as rural as parts of the neighbouring counties of Herefordshire, Worcestershire and Staffordshire. The Wren's Nest in Dudley is world famous for fossils, in particular *Calymene Blumenbachi*, so common in the area it was nick-named the 'Dudley Locust'. It continues to be celebrated today and forms part of the Dudley County Borough Council coat of arms, granted in 1957, and appears nestled between an anchor and a Davy lamp.

The Black Country dialect is almost unique in Britain, partly because of the geography, but also because of the lack of interference from out-side. The traditional factors that affect how people speak and the place names that were adopted were a result of the invasions of the Danes and influence of the Normans. This was not the case in the Black Country and this will be examined later.

There are many products often associated with the Black Country, food being a good example. Black Country faggots, pork scratchings and black pudding are all part of the local diet, and historically 'graypaes' and 'grorty dick', pig's trotters and chitterlings, were on the menu. Iconic products such as Teddy Gray's herbal tablets are still widely available and made in Dudley. The plethora of local breweries that existed in the Black Country is discussed later in the book. There were many more than in other urban areas, and significantly many remained independent much longer than elsewhere. They also provided a greater choice of individual brews than other areas. There was a proportionately large number of pubs, inns and ale houses, which existed to supply home-brewed beer to the miners, foundry workers, chain makers and others. Many opened for long hours to cater for shift workers, and to provide liquid to slake the thirst of those workers who often endured extremely hot and debilitating working conditions. Pubs are not unique, but they played an integral part in the culture and life of the Black Country.

The Dudley coat of arms with the locust is seen here in the centre of the crest. (Author's photograph)

Certain forms of entertainment have strong connections with the Black Country: cock fighting, bull and bear baiting and bare knuckle fighting are all examples. Breeds of animal are also linked with the area: racing pigeons and Staffordshire Bull Terriers being just two examples.

11

Black Country life was rich in other areas too. Local engineers achieved a number of 'firsts', for example, the railway engine *Stourbridge Lion*, built by Stourbridge firm Foster and Rastrick, was the first ever locomotive to run on rails in the USA. In addition, Chance Brothers Glass Works, in Spon Lane, Smethwick, pioneered the manufacture of sheet glass in the 1830s and won a contract to make glass for the Crystal Palace for the 1851 Great Exhibition. The car company Sunbeam produced the first British car to reach 70mph, which was bettered on 29 March 1927 by a 1000hp Sunbeam Mystery, driven by Henry Segrave, and became the first car to top 200mph.

These varied factors all contribute to make the Black Country a vibrant and fascinating area to study, from the start of the Industrial Revolution right through to present times, when the demographic has changed yet again, this time as a result of greater cultural diversity.

Documenting the Workshop of the World

In 2005 the Heritage Lottery Fund project 'Documenting the Workshop of the World' was set up, supported by further funds from the Black Country Consortium. Its objectives were to digitise over 10,000 historic images, charting the development of the Industrial Revolution in the Black Country. In addition, it was responsible for cataloguing a series of archives from businesses across the region. The project ran for three years and employed a number of full-time staff to achieve its objectives. The material worked on comprises a small portion of the total number of images and documents that are contained in the four archive centres at Walsall, Wolverhampton, Sandwell and Dudley. At the conclusion of the project the hardware and software used were left *in situ* to allow further material to be added to the collection in the future.

Over 10,000 images have so far been digitised and many archives catalogued and made available to the public. Some of the company archives include AJS (motor-cycle manufacturers from Wolverhampton), Stewarts and Lloyds (tube makers from Halesowen), William Butler (brewer from Priestfield – later part of Mitchells and Butlers) and John Bradley and Co. (Stourbridge iron manufacturers and coal miners). The work started by the project continues through each of the archive centres.

Chapter 1

IRON AND STEEL

Introduction

This chapter details the development of one of the most important industries in the Black Country, the manufacture of iron and steel. The smelting of iron ore into cast and wrought iron was the catalyst for everything that followed in the Industrial Revolution, and the Black Country had the greatest concentration of heavy industry anywhere in Britain. There were a number of major contributors responsible for the growth of the iron and steel industry, and some of these, such as the Earl of Dudley and Alfred Hickman, are discussed later in this chapter.

In the nineteenth century the West Midlands was described as the 'workshop of the world', known worldwide as a centre for industrial design and innovation. The Black Country played a key role during this period, especially in terms of manufacturing and production. Some of the main industries were nail and chain making around Cradley Heath and elsewhere, boiler making around Netherton and leather making and loriny (a loriner makes and sells bits, bridles, spurs, stirrups, saddle trees and the minor metal items of a horse's harness) in Walsall, to be discussed in more depth in chapter 4. It has already been said that if it wasn't made in the Black Country, it probably wasn't made anywhere!

Early Years

One of the two most important raw materials in the production of iron was iron ore; the other was coal, which is discussed elsewhere. Iron ore was plentiful and widely distributed around the region, usually in the form of iron oxide. Ironstone was found at Birchills, Cockshutts, Delves, Willenhall and James Bridge near Walsall. The smelting of iron had been carried out in Britain before the Roman Conquest and through the ages techniques were modernised and furnaces grew in size. In Walsall, in about 1300, 'Adam the Bloomer' was mentioned in records; probably a smelter of iron, a bloomer (charcoal fire) was used to create a few pounds of iron from ore. In 1377 John Sporier was almost certainly a spur maker in the same area. In the fifteenth century there is evidence of an iron mill in operation near Aldridge, sometime between 1474 and 1495, on land belonging to Simon Monfort. The method use by the bloomer required water to make iron and produced an inferior and less malleable form than that made in a furnace. Wood to make charcoal was also needed, and at this time there were large tracts of forest in the Black Country.

The blast furnace was introduced in Europe in 1500, and this made production of cast iron possible. The higher temperatures in the furnace melted iron ore to produce cast iron, which could then be treated to produce wrought iron. It is believed that the first blast furnace in Britain was located at the Weald in Sussex. Closer to home, in 1561 Lord Paget established the first blast furnace, fuelled by charcoal, near Hednesford on Cannock Chase. During the early years of the seventeenth century eight furnaces were in existence in and around the Black Country at locations such as Cradley, Himley, Rushall and Bromwich; all were charcoal furnaces. Development came swiftly during the seventeenth century. Lord Dudley was granted the rights to mine minerals over a large area; it has been said the rights given to Lord Dudley were far greater than those given to other local lords of the manor, the Earls of Bradford and Dartmouth. The change from bloomeries to blast furnaces did not happen overnight, and bloomeries were still operating well into the seventeenth century.

The best wood for charcoal burning was oak, which was becoming scarce by the seventeenth century. Dud Dudley, an illegitimate son of Edward, Lord Dudley, knew there was a plentiful supply of coal near to the furnace and forges he used at Pensnett Chase, and decided to experiment with its use in smelting. Dud realised that as demand for iron grew charcoal was not going to be available in sufficient quantities to sustain development in iron smelting, so alternative means would be necessary.

In 1619, aged 20, Dudley obtained a licence to use a patent granted to one John Robinson, which was a method of smelting iron using pit-coal. In 1621 he applied to renew this patent in his own name, having had samples of iron made using the process. Dud Dudley produced 'good merchantable iron', eventually manufacturing 7 tons per week. He also used the iron to make: 'all sorts of cast iron wares, as brewing cysterns, pots, morters, and better and cheaper than any made in these nations with charcoal'. Many years later, in 1665, Dudley wrote a book, *Metallum Martis*, about the process, although the description was so muddled that no one has been able to ascertain exactly what he developed. Dudley died, aged 85, and took his secret of smelting iron from 'pit-cole' with him to the grave. There is a memorial to Dud Dudley at St Helen's Church, Worcester.

Another important character in the early development of the iron industry in the Black Country was Richard Foley (1580–1657). The Foleys settled in Stourbridge in 1630, in a building in High Street that is now the Talbot Hotel. Richard, son of a Dudley nailer, also Richard, was to become the most successful ironmaster of his time. By 1657 Foley ironworks across the Black Country accounted for half of the West Midlands's production of iron, and a quarter of the production in England and Wales. Richard was in the right position to grow his business, with good rivers to supply water power, namely the Stour and Tame and their tributaries, as well as excellent supplies of raw materials. There was a plentiful source of woodland to provide wood to make the charcoal needed for smelting. The road system was poor, but was sufficient for Foley's needs and was a relatively cheap means of transport.

Foley began by operating a nailing workshop. He then sold iron as an ironmonger before progressing to leasing forges using capital raised from

The Talbot Hotel, High Street, Stourbridge. This was Richard Foley's home in the town. (Author's photograph)

15

his earlier enterprises. As he made more money he acquired furnaces to supply his forges with iron. Foley also pioneered the slitting, or rod, mill, which turned bar iron into rods suitable for making nails and chain. In about 1627 Foley built his first slitting mill, the greatest advance in the iron industry in the seventeenth century, and this greatly improved productivity and eventually profit. Its rollers produced a thin iron plate, and cutters split the plate into rods ready for the nailer.

The third important character in the early history of the iron industry was John 'Iron Mad' Wilkinson. He constructed an iron works at Bradley, near Bilston, in 1766. Some historians believe this period marks the birth of the Black Country, even if it wouldn't acquire the name for a further eighty years. Demand for local ironstone, limestone and coal increased rapidly as more furnaces and forges were built. Transport links had to develop to meet the demands of industrial growth, which led to the birth of the canals and railways.

One example of the innovation of Black Country engineering was built by the Horseley Iron Company in Tipton. In 1821 the firm constructed the world's first iron steamship, the *Aaron Manby*, named after a partner in the firm. Once built it was transported by canal to London and re-assembled for trials on the River Thames. The press declared it 'the most complete piece of workmanship in the iron way that has ever been witnessed'. The ship sailed to France, where it competed against French boats; it is reported to have been dismantled in France in 1855.

The number of blast furnaces grew steadily, peaking in 1860/1. At this time there were 191 furnaces, both working and closed down, at 66 locations. By the end of 1861 only 108 blast furnaces remained working, but this did not mean that production was slowing down. Bigger and more efficient furnaces were built as smelting methods developed; it was far more efficient for furnaces to increase in size but reduce in number.

During much of the nineteenth century production levels were subject to boom and slump, often dictated by military requirements for armaments and other items necessary for the growth of the British Empire. A classic example of this nature of the industry was the town of Darlaston. In the early part of the nineteenth century, especially during the Napoleonic Wars, Darlaston was a major manufacturer of gun locks. At times of peak production this was very profitable and a good worker could earn £1 a day. This meant that a gunlock maker could earn enough in two days to keep him and his family for a whole week, if he was so inclined. In 1858 a Black Country miner could still only earn between £1 and £1 10s a week, though this was during a slump following the Crimean War. This influx of money meant that Darlaston became the most profitable market in the neighbourhood, but it was not to last. Once the war ended, after the Battle of Waterloo in 1815, demand for gun locks reduced dramatically and wages fell to around 3–4s a day, if there was any work at all.

The website www.measuringworth.com/ppoweruk gives an indication of what money could buy over the years. It covers the period from 1264 to the present day and there are a number of searches and calculators available, depending on the information you require.

The Height of the Industrial Revolution – Round Oak

In 1857 in Brierley Hill one of the most significant iron works opened, the Round Oak Iron Works, established by the first Earl of Dudley and known as 'The Earl's'. A year previously two of the most significant inventions in steel making had been developed. Sir William Siemens, a German immigrant, invented the open-hearth furnace, later a major feature at Round Oak. Also, Sir Henry Bessemer, son of a French refugee, invented a process often called 'converting'. This consisted of blowing air through the molten pig iron inside a suitable vessel, the converter. This oxidised any impurities, which could then be removed. Later in the century both processes were used in the Black Country.

At the time it opened, 'The Earl's' had 28 puddling furnaces, and so compared to similar works elsewhere in the Black Country, with between 10 and 20, it was a much larger operation. The Round Oak initially covered 15 acres and employed 600 men. Griffiths' *Guide to the Iron Trade of Great Britain* (1873) states: 'The Earl of Dudley's iron takes its proper position in the market, and is top of all Staffordshire makes'. The period between 1857 and 1889 were halcyon days at 'The Earl's' in terms of iron production. However, the growth and development in the making of mild steel caused a rethink. In the late 1880s the Dudley family decided to move into steel production.

The project to build a steel plant at Round Oak began in 1890 and the first steel furnace was tapped in 1894. During the project the Earl of Dudley was persuaded to sell Round Oak for £110,000. However, by 1894 the company had gone into liquidation and the works reverted to Lord Dudley, as the mortgage raised to buy it could not be paid. Once back in Dudley possession the plant prospered and continued to develop and expand. By 1897 Lord Dudley had formed a new company, the Earl of Dudley's Round Oak Works Limited, but apart from attending the first board meeting, Lord Dudley left the management to Sir Gilbert Claughton (his agent), John Tryon (solicitor) and George Hatton (steel maker).

Round Oak developed and prospered up to 1914. During the First World War it produced vitally needed steel for the war effort. Following the war there was a short boom but then a deep slump and the Great Depression, and these were difficult times at Round Oak and necessitated tight financial control and re-structuring. Following the Second World War further modernisation was required, and this was completed in 1951. The works was now producing 250,000 tons of steel a year. The Iron and Steel Act 1949 produced a list of companies identified for nationalisation, and this included Round Oak. After a short period of nationalisation from 1951–3, a new Conservative government sold the works for £6,000,000, to Tube Investments Ltd.

Iron and Steel in Bilston

In 1866 the Hickman family acquired Springvale Furnaces Ltd. Developments in steel production were moving the industry forward rapidly. In 1875 two men, Sidney Gilchrist Thomas and his cousin, Percy Gilchrist, discovered a method of removing phosphorus from iron ore, essential in making steel. This method, combined with the Bessemer converter, enabled Sir Alfred Hickman to set up the Staffordshire Steel and Ingot Iron Co. Ltd, including Springvale Works, which turned Bilston from an iron to a steel town. The use of steel was seen as being preferable to cast iron. There had been a number of instances of cast-iron bridges collapsing, for example, the Dee Bridge disaster in 1847, where a train crossing the cast-iron bridge in Chester collapsed with the loss of five lives. It was also a fact that steel rail track lasted more than twenty times longer than iron track. Over a period of time all cast-iron bridges and rail track were replaced with steel.

In 1887 Hickman expanded his operation in Bilston; he installed a Bessemer plant and an experimental open-hearth furnace. By 1897 the Springvale site in Bilston occupied over 200 acres and employed 1,500 men and was known as Bilston Steel Works. Hickman was one of the first in the region to install electricity in his works, allowing 24-hour working to be safely carried out. The twentieth century saw greater modernisation at the plant, which was acquired by Stewarts and Lloyds in 1921. Most of the production was of tube steel, and PLUTO (Pipe Line under the Ocean) was manufactured from this. The pipe line ran under the English Channel and was constructed for the Normandy invasions in 1944 to convey fuel to Allied armies. The line was extended as the Allies advanced through France. A total of 80 miles of the tube steel used was supplied by Stewarts and Lloyds for this project.

Like Round Oak, Stewarts and Lloyds was nationalised in 1951. The nationalisation was also reversed soon after, due to a change in government. During that period modernisation was again on the agenda. In 1954 a new blast furnace was erected at Bilston, and named 'Elisabeth' after the young daughter of one of the senior managers at the works. The furnace, nicknamed 'Lizzy', was the pride of Bilston Steel Works. Its capacity was 275,000 tons of steel a year, and in its lifetime it produced 5½ million tons of pig iron. However, the industry was facing a downturn, which would mark the end of the Black Country's focal position in the industrial arena.

The Decline and Demise of the Steel Industry

Both Round Oak and Stewarts and Lloyds were nationalised for a second time in 1966 when they became part of the British Steel Corporation (BSC). This followed heated debates in Parliament, with MPs expressing polarised views about whether nationalisation would help the industry. Competition from abroad, for example from South Africa, was having an effect on British steel companies.

Decisions made at BSC level caused the demise of Bilston Steel Works. While it was a major plant in the West Midlands, it was small compared with other BSC sites. This did not cause a problem while customers were able to order from individual BSC plants, and Bilston remained very profitable. However, in 1976 a central ordering system was implemented. This and the general downturn in the industry, including greater competition from Europe, led to the closure of 'Elisabeth' in November 1977. This almost halved steel production at Bilston overnight and turned the operation into a loss-making one, ending a 416-year tradition of blast furnaces in the town. Electric furnaces continued to operate, but there were to be no more blast furnaces in the Black Country. In 1979, despite a rigorous campaign to save it, Bilston Steel Works closed, leading to a great increase in unemployment in the area. The site was cleared and handed over to the National Coal Board, which began open-cast mining there. During this operation evidence of previous mining was unearthed, including the remains of bell pits and older small coal workings. When all available coal had been extracted the site was restored and used for housing, part of the new arterial route known today as the Black Country Route, and an industrial estate.

Closure was a bitter pill for the area to swallow. BSC forecast that, from its point of view, work would simply transfer to BSC Rotherham.

History has shown that this did not happen and much of the work went abroad. The open-hearth furnace was also seen as being out of date, and despite the fact that arguments were put forward that they could be as efficient as electric furnaces, these were lost. One of the staunchest campaigners to save Bilston Steel Works was Dennis Turner MP, now Lord Turner. Ironically, he later watched the hub of the London Eye being transported down the Thames – it had been made in Hungary in an open-hearth furnace.

The ultimate fate of Round Oak seemed almost inevitable, considering what had happened at Bilston. At its peak thousands were employed at 'The Earl's', but times were changing. In 1970 there had been major investment at Round Oak, with the installation of two new electric furnaces. However, on 23 December 1982, despite a fierce argument about profitability led by local MP John Blackburn, it finally closed, with the loss of 1,286 jobs. The plant was demolished in 1984.

The site had been designated an Enterprise Zone in 1981 and after Round Oak had been demolished the site was redeveloped as the Merry Hill Centre, one of the largest shopping centres in Britain. It has provided thousands of jobs in the area and has transformed the landscape of Brierley Hill.

The closures of Bilston and Round Oak heralded the end of major steel production in the area. Other smaller concerns remained in business, and there is also plenty of manufacturing going on in the Black Country today, but the process of smelting iron and producing steel is now a distant memory.

Working Conditions

A foundry was obviously a very hot and dirty place to work and it could also be very dangerous – accidents and industrial diseases were commonplace. On 15 October 1875 a disaster occurred at the Green Lane Iron Works in Walsall. Men were working in the foundry and molten iron was being tapped (poured) into the moulds used for making pig iron. A hole at the bottom of the furnace (a tuyere) suddenly burst, covering workers in the vicinity with molten metal and red-hot ashes. Such was the extent of the blast that all the windows in the office 40yd away were shattered. A total of three men died at the scene and a further ten died later as a result of severe burns, while another four received serious injuries but survived. At the nearby cottage hospital a ward was devoted to treating the wounded, and surgeons were promptly in attendance. The

Walsall Free Press (16 October 1875) listed the names of all the casualties. Devoted nursing care was provided by Sister Dora, who is discussed later in the book.

Further Information

One of only three Bessemer converters still in existence in the world can be seen at Kelham Island Museum in Sheffield. It was used by BSC in Workington until 1975, and was transferred to the museum in 1978 as an example of the revolutionary steel-making process that was first developed in Sheffield. See the Kelham Island Museum website for more information at: www.simt.co.uk.

There are a number of sources of information should you want to research Bilston Steel Works further. Two recommended websites are: www.localhistory.scit.wlv.ac.uk/articles/BilstonDirectory/SteelWorks/steelworks00.htm and www.wolverhamptonhistory.org.uk/work/industry/steel. Many useful documents, maps and photographs can be found at Wolverhampton Archives and Local Studies Service.

Round Oak Iron and Steel is also well documented and many records are held at Dudley Archives. Many of the Earl of Dudley's estate records are also kept there. There was a quarterly company magazine published from 1956 to 1979 called the *Acorn*, which can be difficult to access but does contain many references to employees with entries and photographs of significant events, as well as articles about Round Oak and the iron and steel industry in general. In 1978 a newspaper called the *Oakleaf* was started at Round Oak to provide more immediate information to workers. This was a monthly publication and some editions are available via Dudley Archives.

There have been some useful books written about the iron industry around the Black Country. Recent publications include Ray Shill's *South Staffordshire Ironmasters* and Roy Peacock's *The Seventeenth Century Foleys: Iron and Wealth Vision 1580–1716*. Collie Knox's *Steel at Brierley Hill (1857–1957)* chronicles the first 100 years of Round Oak; it was published by Round Oak and although it is long out of print, it is available through Dudley Library Service.

Researching Your Ancestors

Throughout this book newspapers are highlighted as valuable research tools. One relevant website can be found at: www.newsplan.co.uk. Its

West Midlands database gives details of some 1,100 newspaper titles published in counties including Shropshire, Staffordshire, Warwickshire, Worcestershire and the Metropolitan Boroughs of Birmingham, Coventry, Dudley, Sandwell, Solihull, Walsall and Wolverhampton. Entries include details of main titles, name changes and information on libraries and record offices where copies are held. Entries also indicate if copies are held at the British Library Newspaper Collection in London and also whether the newspapers are held in bound format or on microfilm.

From 2005 a three-year project, supported by Heritage Lottery Funding, called 'Documenting the Workshop of the World' saw the digitisation of over 10,000 historical images and the cataloguing of a series of business records from across the Black Country. These records chronicle the important role the Black Country played during the Industrial Revolution. The catalogue is searchable online through the Black Country History website at: www.blackcountryhistory.org and documents can be viewed at the relevant local archive. The catalogue also includes many photographs from across the region, which are also available to view online. Another useful website is the British Steel Archive Collection at: www.britishsteelcollection.org.uk. While it does not currently have much relevance to the steel industry in the Black Country, material is added on a regular basis.

Employment records may be more difficult to find, and only of use if you know where your ancestor worked. The National Archives (TNA) website is an essential tool for all aspects of research, not just iron and steel, as you will discover later. This site identifies resources from around the country on your given subject of research. It can be found at: www.nationalarchives.gov.uk.

As with many Black Country occupations, historical job titles may need to be 'de-coded', and those in the iron and steel industry are no exception. The table below gives examples, but is not an exhaustive list. Once a job has been identified the next step will be to find possible employers near to where your ancestor lived. One useful resource is historic maps; many are available in collections at the archives, and maps for certain periods and areas are also available for purchase. Maps may identify local employers by name, or a 'works', without identifying a trade. One useful website is: www.old-maps.co.uk, where you can view old maps online; for example, there are seventeen maps you can consult for Bilston, which can be viewed online and also purchased. From the maps you may find reference to named companies in the area and more information can be searched for at the relevant archive, where you may find company documents.

Iron and Steel Occupations

Job Title	Description
Bloomsmith (fourteenth and fifteenth centuries)	Worked the blooms (impure form of iron in the early stage of production) on a hearth, before passing it to the brandsmith
Brandsmith	Completed the process started by the bloomsmith, hammering iron on an anvil into a bar ready for the smithy
Founder	One who casts metal
Ironmaster	Manufacturer of iron
Puddler	One of two men working a puddling furnace. One was in charge, the other, the 'underhand puddler', was an assistant
Shingler	Workman at a shingling hammer (used to press the slag from within the puddling iron)

23

Chapter 2

MINING

Introduction

The first incidences of mining in the Black Country date from the late thirteenth century, in the Manor of Sedgley, Oldswinford and Halesowen. This chapter explores the records you can use to help trace and develop a picture of your mining ancestors. The emphasis is on coal mining, as this was the main form of mining in the Black Country. The topics covered are mining as an occupation, the risks of mining and miners' disputes. In each of these areas there are useful records available, and these are discussed in some depth. You can also experience what mining was like in the nineteenth century through a number of websites, and the main ones are listed here.

The geology of the Black Country provides a rich legacy in the Staffordshire thick coal-seam. This comprised a number of beds of coal, varying from 8ft to 14ft in parts. The best coal was found around Dudley and Oldbury, where it was worked to its greatest depth of 30ft. In the north it was cut off east to west by the Bentley Fault, but eventually rose again to become the Cannock Field to the north. To the east and west of Dudley the seam thinned and broke into a number of seams, which were less economic to mine.

The first recorded mention of the use of coal was in the twelfth century, mainly in the north of England. It was taken from where coal-seams came to the surface. The South Staffordshire thick coal-seam (30ft) was a unique feature in England, and was vital to the region's development before and during the Industrial Revolution. The first references to coal mining in the Black Country were in the Manor of Sedgley, from 1271 to 1291, Oldswinford in 1291 and Coombs Wood (Halesowen) in 1307, when the Abbott of Hales was granted the lease of a mine. It was clear that limestone was also being used at about the same time, and the earliest example of it in a building is at Dudley Castle and Priory, which date from the twelfth century. The limestone was located in Dudley, together with plentiful coal supplies and led to the town being at the heart of the Industrial Revolution in the Black Country.

Dr Plot, an English naturalist and Fellow of the Royal Society, wrote in 1686 about mining in Wednesbury, where he observed miners digging a trench to remove the topsoil before digging the coal beneath their feet. In Netherton men were able to pick up a seam and dig into the hillside, often up to 100yd. Deeper coal mining began in the late 1600s. Again, Dr Plot observed a scene in Wednesbury, where he noted 11 acres of 'wild-fire' caused by burning slack underground. Slack was not worth removing during mining, and as it burns easily underground fires were common.

Mining was a tough industry, accident rates were high and many accidents led to fatalities. It also took its toll on workers: 'His stature is diminutive, his figure disproportionate and misshapen, his legs being much bowed ... His arms are long, and oddly suspended ... nor is his appearance healthful' (John Roby Leifchild, leading evangelical minister; in the 1850s Leifchild was a visiting Government Commissioner to coal mines).

As demand for coal grew new methods had to be found to obtain it. The landscape of the region was about to undergo a massive trans-formation as the Industrial Revolution gained pace. The mining industry fought a constant battle against water and flooding was common in mines. In 1712 a steam pumping engine, with a cylinder and piston, was used for the first time at a mine somewhere between Dudley and Tipton. It was built by Cornish engineer Thomas Newcomen and was erected to pump water. It consumed a lot of coal, so it was ideally suited for use in the Black Country. A full-sized replica of the engine can be found in the Black Country Living Museum (BCLM), the location of which is probably not far from where the original engine once operated.

The following comment was recorded following a visit to a Wednesbury pit, 'The whole country round about, seems turned inside out, it is worked in all directions, for ironstone, coal and limestone' (*Osborne's Guide to the Grand Junction, or Birmingham, Liverpool and Manchester Railway* (1838)).

Industry developed where coal was plentiful, preferably close to lime-stone and iron ore. Foundries developed around the seam and, as demand grew for raw materials, mining was set to undergo its own revolution. The main mining areas in the north were Sedgley, Coseley, Bilston and Wednesbury; Dudley at the very heart; and in the south Netherton and Halesowen were significant centres. The mining industry effectively ended in the Black Country with the closure of Baggeridge Colliery in March 1968. Baggeridge was the last of the deep mines, and once it closed there were only a few open-cast mines left working. As mentioned in

Replica of Newcomen's engine, on display at the Black Country Living Museum. (Author's photograph)

chapter 1, following the closure of Bilston Steel Works in the early 1980s there was a short period when deep mining returned.

The Butty and the Truck System

Many mines in the nineteenth century were owned by major landowners, such as the Earls of Dudley, Dartmouth or Bradford. The butty was the middleman who contracted with the mining company to deliver an agreed tonnage of coal to the pithead, hiring and paying his own labour. The truck system ('Tommy Truck') was born out of stiff competition for 'butty contracts', resulting in low profit margins. In order that the butties could make money they often paid workers in 'Tommy Notes', which could only be redeemed for goods at the butty's own shop or in the butty's public house. Prices here were higher than elsewhere and helped the butty maximise his profits. The butty system meant there was a lack of consistency in terms and conditions of employment. Some employers provided benefits for their workers; Lord Dudley was one such example. Good employers took responsibility when things went wrong, as happened in the Nine Locks mining disaster in 1879. There were two butties operating at the mine, but as soon as things began to go wrong Lord Dudley's agents took over running the rescue operation. The butties were involved, but responsibility was accepted by the agents.

Apart from the truck system, other aspects of the way the butty organised and carried out his work were heavily criticised. Some techniques used were wasteful in terms of miners' health and lives and were economically disastrous. Some would supply the minimum of timber to build roof supports, and apprentices were used and abused. Many butties also had other business interests, some not related to mining. He may have been administering to the coalfield as merchant, operating as an insurer or even keeping a brothel. He may also have been the owner of a public house. The 1854 Select Committee on Accidents in Coal Mines was very critical of the butty system nationally.

In 1860, travel writer Walter White was touring in the Black Country. He asked a miner whether 'the butty is hired to swear at the doggy, and the doggy to swear at the men?' (Walter White, *All Around the Wrekin*, 1860). This was confirmed by the miner, who described the Saturday afternoon pay ritual at the butty's public house, where 6*d* a week was deducted from wages for the beer the men were going to drink that

Racecourse Colliery at the Black Country Living Museum. (Author's photograph)

afternoon. He was asked about miners who were teetotal, and was told they had to pay the 6*d* as well, whether they drank beer or not.

There was widespread opposition to the system in the second half of the nineteenth century. After 1870 the structure of the mining industry began to change: unions and men opposed the system and miners demanded direct employment on piece-work. Legal cases and new legislation helped facilitate this change, for example Regina v Cope (1867) placed responsibility for safety in the mines firmly on the mine owner and not the butty. The Mines Act of 1872 stipulated that every colliery had to employ qualified and certified mine managers. The Mining Inspectorate was also more active, which led to a reduction in the use of the butty system. By the turn of the twentieth century only a minority of small pits were run by butties, fewer than 2,000 miners in total. The system continued to operate in the Midlands, on a diminishing scale, until the early 1930s.

Children in the Mines

It is important to bear in mind that, especially in the mid-nineteenth century, many young children had jobs in the mines. There are examples of boys and girls as young as 6 being employed, by age 8 many boys worked underground and by 16 boys could be employed in the same jobs as adults. The Children's Employment Commission 1842 examined conditions for children working in mines: '... went to work when he was six years and a half old and was employed to carry picks to be repaired. He continued at this work about a year and a half, and then went down into the pit'. By 16 or 17 a boy was considered competent to carry out any job in the mine.

It was not only boys who were employed in mines: 'On the banks of the canals in Staffordshire are seen many girls engaged in loading the boats with coals. These girls are substantially, though coarsely, clothed, and the head and neck more particularly protected from the cold. The work is laborious but not beyond their strength.' The report does not identify the ages of the girls seen working, but they are probably similar to the boys.

Graham's Act of 1844 legislated to make children half-time workers; it also stipulated a condition that safety fencing be fitted to dangerous machinery. Conditions for children working in the mines varied, with some employers enforcing a rule of no swearing underground and that prayers should be said. Others were not so considerate to their youngest employees. In 1903 children were able to leave school at 12, as long as they had a 'Labour Certificate', which showed that they had reached a certain standard, confirmed by examination, in reading, writing and arithmetic.

Mining Records

It is perhaps ironic that some of the main sources of documentary evidence about mining ancestors are reports about their death, injury or involvement in a work-related accident or incident. Personal records of mines and employees may still exist, but are only available at local archives; tracking down the employment history of a mining ancestor is likely to require extensive research. There were large numbers of pits in any locality, some very small, and a mine's 'lifespan' was determined by size and the amount of coal that could be economically extracted. Leases on mines were often signed for between four and twenty-one years. This meant miners had to be 'upwardly mobile' within their area, moving from pithead to pithead to follow the work. There was also movement to other parts of the country, and indeed abroad, as mining was a skill often required elsewhere. Emigration and immigration are examined in chapter 5.

One place to begin your research is the census, which will identify your ancestor's occupation and also where he lived. The national census began in 1801 and was repeated every ten years. The 1841 census is the first one of use to family history researchers, and can be accessed at archives and online. Maps of the area where your ancestor lived may also identify names and locations of mines. Be careful to find a map that corresponds as closely as possible to the census year (or years) you are interested in. There are some useful coal-mining maps on the website of the Coalmining History Resource Centre at: www.cmhrc.co.uk/site/home. There are also reprints of old Ordnance Survey maps available from two companies: Alan Godfrey Maps and Cassini, which both have websites and often attend events such as family history fairs. The Old-Maps website at: www.old-maps.co.uk is also helpful.

Church records are another important way of tracing ancestors and their occupations. From the early nineteenth century the register of baptisms may include information such as the number of people in a family, father's occupation and parish of origin for both parents. This last item might help if you believe an ancestor was an immigrant to the Black Country. Many miners, for example, came from Wales to work in the region, and there is evidence of significant numbers of people born in

Wales settling in Dudley, Bilston, Rowley Regis and Tipton in census returns, all giving their occupation as miner. The burial register may also help to provide information including the place and date of death and details of any spouse. The date and place of death may be most useful if your ancestor was killed at work.

Some detective work is likely to be required in order to go further, including a trip to an archive. Each archive holds series of maps showing mine locations and records of mines, which should identify the owner, any lease on the mine and possibly the manager, as well as the date it opened and maybe some employment records. All Black Country archives have some form of index system, catalogued by subject, location and name. This may help identify relevant documents to examine, including estate records. For example, at Dudley Archives the Dudley Estate records are held and the Earl of Dudley owned many mines around Dudley, including well-known ones such as Baggeridge. Some of the records you can access from the Dudley Estate are leases and tenancy agreements, accounts, canal, railway and building plans and sales of property.

The census return, and indeed other documents, may mention a number of mining occupations; there were no hard and fast rules about what a job might have been called. Below is a list, not exhaustive, of mining jobs, together with a short description of each post. Job titles changed through the years, and it is beyond the scope of this book to cover them all. A useful website that explains census-related job titles is: www.familytreeservice.co.uk/census%20occupations.html.

Mining Jobs

Job Title	Description
(Accredited) Agent	Chief official of a large mine, or group of mines under the same ownership, holder of a mining licence
Bandsman or Onsetter	Labourer working with a band of men
Banker, Banksman or Browman	Person who controlled loading and unloading of the cage at the pithead
Bearers	Early term for boys, girls or women who carried coal underground in baskets on their backs
Bellman	Man who worked on the conveyor or rope haulage signalling system

Job Title	Description
Butty (elsewhere called a Charter Master)	The butty was a sub-contractor. He bought the tools, carts, horses etc. and was contracted to deliver coal into wagons for a price per ton. Several men could have worked a butty system at a mine and shared the investment
Chandler	In early mining he was employed at the mine to make candles
Chargeman or Chargehand	A working foreman, not a mine official
Collier or Hewer	General underground worker
Coal Stower	Loaded hand-picked coal into wagons by hand
Deputy or Deputies	Responsible for setting timber for safety purposes. Also deputised as managers in the area of the pit they were responsible for
Doggy	Petty foreman in a mine
Filler	Person who loaded coal by hand at the face
Haulier	In charge of a pit pony
Heaver or Holer	Coal cutter or digger, broke down coal ready for a filler to load the tubs
Ostler or Horse Fettler	Responsible for the welfare of mine horses
Powder Monkey	Usually a small boy who carried the powder box and kept tally of how much had been used
Wagon Trimmer	Responsible for proper loading of wagons; levelling coal on wagons; examination and top trimming of coal in wagons

Mining Risks

Mining was a risky occupation and workers often faced the twin hazards of water and fire. In 1900, for example, it was estimated that some 40 million tons of coal lay waterlogged underground in the Black Country. Underground fires were also common, although some never actually broke out in flames and were known as 'Blue Flies' because of the blue-tinted gaseous vapours they gave off by night. Parish registers from the eighteenth century are testimony to the problem of underground fires. In 1731 it was recorded in Wednesbury that a collier was 'most dismally scorched and roasted to death by the Hellish Wildfire, June ye 20th'. There are other entries attributing death to 'wildfire' or 'firing of the damp'.

In the nineteenth century accidents were common and working conditions tough, while safety law was not as comprehensive or effective as today. A Royal Commission appointed Commissioners to examine conditions in the coalfields around the country, to gather evidence and report their findings to Parliament. These reports can be viewed online at: www.cmhrc.co.uk/site/literature/royalcommissionreports, with the South Staffordshire report of most relevance to the Black Country, although the others make interesting reading. In 1843 the Mines Inspectorate was formed. Some of their records are available at TNA, and it is necessary to visit to view these. During this period there were many examples of accidents, brutality, lung disease, long hours and dangerous working conditions and practices. Up until the turn of the century lighting was by candle and floods and fires were still risks: 'Fires in mines may arise from the spontaneous combustion of iron pyrites, or of the slack or small coal itself' (*Children's Employment Commission* (1842), South Staffordshire).

In 1894 there was a fire in a colliery in Wednesbury that lasted until at least 1899 (when the last information about the fire was recorded). The fire began under Old Park Road, probably as a result of spontaneous combustion or weakening of the underground roof causing friction. The colliery had to be closed and abandoned, in the hope it would burn itself out. Months later local residents found the ground cracking and pungent acrid smoke and steam began issuing forth. In February 1897 the road completely gave way, exuding flames and smoke into the air. The road had to be barricaded for safety and crowds flocked to see this extraordinary sight. As subsidence continued to lower the level of the road it was totally closed and a watchman was appointed by the corporation to oversee the area.

On the night of Wednesday 14 April 1898 disaster struck. A policeman saw the watchman leave his hut to warn three men wandering close to one of the holes. The officer walked towards where the men had been to make sure they had moved away. When he turned round the watchman was missing, believed fallen into a cavity from which dense smoke emanated. The alarm was raised and a young constable, Richard Goldby, volunteered to descend the hole by ladder. Goldby could not

Subterranean fire, Wednesbury, 1894. (*Blackcountryman* magazine, Autumn 1971)

see the watchman, but could feel him. Overcome by smoke, he returned to the surface and prepared to descend again, this time with a rope. He was able to tie the rope round the watchman and the men were hauled to the surface. The watchman was found to be dead, with terrible burns to the face and head. The officer was overcome by poisonous fumes and taken to hospital, where he made a full recovery. He was recognised for his bravery and presented with a medal by the Prince of Wales. In January 1899 it was recorded that the fire was still burning fiercely and that several houses and buildings had collapsed; it was agreed that this was the worst fire of its kind ever experienced in the Black Country. This account comes from the Methodist prize book *Good Words* (1901), edited by D MacLeod, one of His Majesty's Chaplains.

The Inspector of mines and collieries only had limited powers, but undertook many prosecutions and made recommendations on training, accident reporting, provision of pithead baths and suitable habitation for mine workers. In 1850 inspectors were able to enter and inspect mine premises. The table below lists significant mining accidents in the Black Country.

Mining Accidents in the Black Country where Five or More People were Killed

Date	Colliery	Location	Number Killed
1806	Unnamed	Dudley	8 or 10
October 1821	Ebenezer	West Bromwich	6
2 November 1835	Pumphouse	Dudley Port	16
February 1837		Oldbury	5
30 August 1843	Holly Hall	Dudley	6
19 August 1844	Five Ways	Rowley Regis	11
15 April 1846	Fire Clay Pit	Bilston	5
17 November 1846	Rounds Green New Pit	Oldbury	20
9 February 1848	Heathfield	Wolverhampton	16
26 June 1849	Great Bridge	Friary Field, Dudley	15–25
November 1850	Willingsworth	Sedgley	5
16 June 1852	Bunkers Hill	Bilston	5
26 April 1853	Old Park	Dudley	11
31 May 1853	Rosehill	Willenhall	Unknown
20 June 1856	Old Park	Dudley	8
13 August 1856	Ramrod Hall	Oldbury	11
10 September 1857	Gwane	Dudley	9
30 May 1862	Old Bradley	Bilston	7
11 January 1864	Bridge End	Pensnett	6
16 November 1864	Withymore	Rowley Regis	8
9 February 1865	Salt Well	Dudley	6
1 November 1866	Homer Hill	Cradley	12
2 March 1867	Clattershall	Stourbridge	5
12 November 1867	Homer Hill	Cradley	12
11 March 1868	Clattershall	Stourbridge	5
23 November 1871	Blacklane	West Bromwich	Unknown
23 July 1874	Titford Long Meadow	Oldbury	5
12 November 1879	Shortheath	Willenhall	6
6 September 1884	Hall End	West Bromwich	7
4 March 1908	Hamstead	Great Barr	25
22 October 1915	Pennant Hill	Dudley	5
18 March 1929	Coombs Wood	Halesowen	8
1 October 1930	Grove	Brownhills	14

Source: Coalmining History Resource Centre at: www.cmhrc.co.uk/site/disasters/index.html

On the Coalmining History Resource Centre website there are lists of accidents from 1600 to the present day. There are further documents outlining what information is available about individual accidents and

34

you can search for names of people killed or injured in accidents; clicking on the name takes you to the details about their accident.

Local records and information on accidents includes inquest records and reports in local newspapers, both at the time of the incident through to the inquest. Some accidents resulted in an official enquiry, the report of which may contain personal details. The level of reporting in newspapers varies, but may include details of the funerals of any workers killed and often quite graphic descriptions of the incident. Newspaper information sometimes includes details of next of kin as well as family names and their addresses. It may be useful to check church records, or there may be some form of memorial still in existence relating to the incident. Later events may have personal oral or written records. For example, an account of the disaster at Hamstead Colliery in 1908 can be accessed via the Hamstead Miners Memorial Trust website at: http://miners.b43.co.uk; it includes photographs and details of a book that can be purchased.

Hamstead Colliery Disaster, 1908

On Wednesday 4 March 1908, at around 5pm, a fire broke out near the bottom of the downcast shaft of Hamstead Colliery. It was thought that the fire started in a wooden box containing candles. There were thirty-one men underground when it started, and only six escaped before poisonous fumes built up in the roadways. Telephone equipment had been taken down into the mine by the workers, but it had been reported that the system had been out of order on Monday 2 March. On the morning of the accident signals were heard at the surface, but no one underground had sent these. This may have indicated something was wrong with the wiring, possibly a short circuit, and that this caused the subsequent disaster. At about 5.30pm William Carter saw smoke coming from the underground roads and men went to investigate the cause. The smell was like that of burning rubber, such as the type used to insulate the underground wires for the telephone system and lighting. Then the electric lights went out, leaving the men in total darkness.

Carter could see flames at the bottom of the pit and the men made a rush for the cage to escape the fire. Carter allowed eight or nine onto the first cage (the normal limit was six), and he and the remainder went up in the second. Carter shouted along the roadway for the other men, but got no response. The fire alarm was raised on the surface at 6pm by the returning men; columns of smoke were now coming out of the upshaft. The manager, Mr Waterhouse, arrived at 7.30pm and decided, because of the smoke, that no one should be allowed into the shaft and HM Inspector of Mines was informed.

It took a week for the mine to clear of fumes. Mine rescue teams from around the country made attempts to rescue the trapped men, but their efforts failed. A week after the accident fourteen bodies were recovered, while another six were found a day later. A total of twenty-five men died. The colliery lost a total of 114 men between 1875 and 1965; the 1908 incident was the largest single loss of life.

A Distressing Colliery Accident

At Lock's Lane Pit, Brierley Hill, at 2am on the morning of Tuesday 16 March 1869 water suddenly flooded the pit, trapping ten men, three boys and six horses underground. As a result two men went down in the lift to investigate, the engineer having seen steam coming from the shaft. They ascertained that it was steam and that there was no fire. The mine pumps were immediately activated, removing 300 tons of water per hour. The Earl of Dudley's agents arrived quickly at the scene to take charge, while enormous crowds gathered to watch events unfold. During the first day it was established that the water level was not falling. Work commenced on digging a passage from the nearby Robin Hood pit. Attempts were made to descend to search for the missing men, but the rescuers' lamps were extinguished by poisonous gases (choke damp). At this time it was feared that the men and boys had died.

On Sunday, in the early hours when it was much quieter, hopes were restored when shouting was heard from the trapped men. Rescue efforts were increased and large quantities of water and lime were thrown down one shaft to nullify the choke damp in the other. Rescuers were able to descend safely and contact was made with the men. A raft was used to rescue five of the six miners in one area, but there was bad news about the sixth, William Ashman. He had apparently been overcome by madness, taken off his clothes and run into the workings; nothing had been heard from him for three days. The other seven were deeper in the mine, and in the early hours of Monday morning the rescuers' efforts were rewarded with shouts from them, and they were brought safely to the surface.

The body of William Ashman was recovered later. At the subsequent inquest, evidence was heard that his lungs were black and that there was partly chewed coal in his stomach. The conclusion was that he had died from breathing impure air. A few days after this incident another man, William Haskin, died in the same pit. This was as a result of a fall of coal as he was removing a 'tree' of coal, which is left in place for safety while a section is excavated. This was a dangerous task that had led to a number of deaths previously. When recovered his body was found to have been 'shockingly mangled' by the coal fall.

Striking Miners

During the Industrial Revolution there were regular industrial disputes. This was not peculiar to the Black Country, but business and life in the region were affected from time to time by strikes and riots.

Miners were among the workers affected by the 'boom and slump' cycles that dogged the nineteenth century. After the Crimean War ended in 1858, for example, there was a slump, and strikes and riots were common. Hardship for mining families was a catalyst for strikes, and a cut in the weekly wage of 1s (between 3 and 5 per cent) was more than enough to trigger action. Men went on strike from July to October, although not all workers were involved. The butty system meant there was a lack of consistency in terms and conditions of employment. Some employers provided benefits for their workers – Lord Dudley was one such employer, and his workers were protected from the iniquities of the truck system. These benefits in the Dudley area meant that fewer workers went on strike in 1858. A different situation existed elsewhere, for example, in Oldbury, where most miners went on strike and persuaded their Kingswinford colleagues to do the same.

Further examples of disorder are the 1831 riots, which highlighted the inequities of the truck system, and the 1921 Coal Strike, which took place during one of the worst depressions of the early twentieth century and ultimately hastened the decline of the coal industry in the region. The 1831 riots arose because of wages. At this time the truck system was being debated in Parliament, and resulted in the Truck Act of the same year. The disturbances were not restricted to miners, and nail makers were equally affected. The riots gained a lot of newspaper coverage, for example, in *Aris's Birmingham Gazette* and the *Wolverhampton Chronicle and Staffordshire Advertiser*. These newspapers can be read at Birmingham and Wolverhampton archives. The Newsplan website at: www.newsplan. co.uk is a useful online resource which contains both newspapers.

The background of the 1921 Coal Strike was the First World War (1914–18). During the war the government 'virtually' nationalised the coal industry and paid very good prices for coal. This led to miners receiving higher wages during the war. However, after the war demand for coal fell, as did output, but costs rose and this hit coal exports in particular.

Miners' wages had risen by 78 per cent since 1914, but prices had risen 120 per cent in the same period. Another factor was that the coal industry across Europe recovered quickly following the end of the war. The 1921 strike began on 1 April and lasted for three months, and ultimately brought the nationalisation of the coal industry a step closer.

The strike caused closures across the region. Within a week of it starting Cochrane and Co. at Woodside had shut down, putting 100 men out of work. The *Dudley Chronicle* (9 April 1921) reported: 'Incalculable damage has already been done and if some move is not made which will restart the colliery pumps within the next 24 hours South Staffordshire will cease to be a great coal producing area.' Across the Black Country distress funds were set up to provide food as the strike developed. At Old Hill soup kitchens were organised, as was the distribution of bread. There were also clashes with police and on 4 May 1921, for example, at New Hawne Colliery in Halesowen strikers tried to prevent slack being moved from mounds for delivery to works. Across the Black Country there were many arrests and subsequent court appearances.

Towards the end of the dispute public sympathy for the miners began to wane – unemployment had risen during the dispute and coal was in

The main building at the New Hawne Colliery. The site is very overgrown and difficult to reach but it is one of very few colliery buildings that remain in the Black Country. (Author's photograph)

short supply. The strike was to do with wages, especially demands for more pay not linked to productivity. The rise in unemployment was due in part to workers losing their jobs in industry because coal was not available, furnaces had to be blown out and workers were laid off. The strike became a major contributor to the decline of the coal industry in the Black Country, especially in Tipton and Old Hill. With no miners working and no fuel to run the water pumps, many pits flooded. Some pits would never re-open because of the investment required to make them ready for extracting coal again.

Mining Unions

The first mining union was the United Association of Colliers, founded in the north east of England in 1823. The first national union was the Miners' Association of Great Britain and Ireland, which was formed in 1841. Although it was short-lived, others soon emerged, principally in Yorkshire. In 1888 the Miners' Federation of Great Britain was established. A history of mining unions can be found on the website of the National Union of Mineworkers at: www.num.org.uk. A more general history of unions is available on the website of the Trades Union Congress at: www.tuc.org.uk. Here there is also a link to the University of Warwick Library, which houses the TUC archive of records with some material dating back to about 1920: www.warwick.ac.uk/services/library/mrc/ead/292col.htm.

Mining Diseases

As well as the risk of accident and injury miners were exposed to a variety of diseases. The environment underground was hostile and this, coupled with the nature of coal mining, could result in a number of medical conditions. Some of these are described below.

Melanosis of the lungs was first described as a disease that arose from coal mining by Gregory in 1831. It was attributed to blasting with gunpowder, or inhaling soot from miners' oil lamps. Another condition was aptly named 'Black Spit', identified in 1833 in men who had worked for fifty years as coal miners. Men's lungs were deteriorating and their phlegm was 'black as printers' ink'. As the destruction of the lungs progressed more black phlegm was produced. Symptoms included shortness of breath and a dry, hacking cough. Dust in the lungs was another condition affecting the respiratory system. Miners throughout the nineteenth century were forced to continue working with this ailment until they became extremely ill. They needed their wages and there was no compensation available until 1928, when miners who were totally disabled were able to claim a weekly pension or a lump sum.

Another problem that affected underground workers was nystagmus, uncontrolled movement of the eyes, which was alleviated when electric lighting was introduced into mines. Finally, bursitis was another common condition and affected joints because of constant pressure through leaning or kneeling for long periods at work. It was often ignored until complications occurred and pain was felt.

Conditions did improve in the twentieth century with more use of mechanical equipment. This in itself often led to conditions that we still hear about today, such as vibration white finger and carpal tunnel syndrome.

Experiencing Mining Life

While the mining industry has declined greatly during the latter half of the twentieth century, and methods have changed beyond all recognition, there are places where you can experience what it was like to be a miner. Close at hand is the BCLM (see chapter 9). Here you can visit authentic

An underground scene from Racecourse Colliery at the Black Country Living Museum.
(Courtesy of the BCLM)

homes where workers lived, and, probably more importantly, there is a mine on site, the Racecourse Colliery, which you can enter as part of a guided tour. This gives an insight into the life of a miner, and the museum also has a library (access by appointment) that holds colliery ledgers and account books.

Further afield is the Apedale Heritage Centre, near Newcastle-Under-Lyme in Staffordshire (see chapter 9). Here there is a typical miner's cottage, artefacts, a mine tour and an above-ground coal-seam. For more information visit the centre's website at: www.apedale.co.uk. Another museum that is highly recommended is the National Coal Mining Museum near Wakefield; www.ncm.org.uk. This free museum allows you to descend a deep mine, one of the oldest in existence. There is also a library containing material relating to disasters, conditions, welfare and much more. Archival information, including employment records, is not held, and local archives should be approached for this kind of material. The library has an online search facility which should identify if there are documents you may be interested in. Although these items can be viewed online, it is best to visit the library in person.

Further Information

TNA has a wealth of material available relating to coal mining, and the dedicated coal-mining records section can be accessed at: www.national archives.gov.uk/records/research-guides/coal-mining.htm#17988. Records span the history of coal mining, the period of both world wars, colliery records, mines inspectorate reports and much more.

Local archives can help with research into your mining ancestors. A good place to begin is at: www.blackcountryhistory.org.uk. Some specific examples of documents held at the various archives are:

Dudley	Colliery workmen's pay books (1848–1945), twenty-two volumes
Staffordshire	South Staffordshire NCB records
Staffordshire University	Journals, maps, surveys and books

If you want to be involved in a web forum, where you can ask questions and receive information from others who have an interest in coal mining, Ancestry maintains a coalminer's mailing list for anyone whose ancestors were coalminers in Britain or the USA. To subscribe send an email with the title 'subscribe' to: coalminers-l-request@rootsweb.com.

There is plenty of written material available on mining. Particularly useful publications are David Tonks' *My Ancestor was a Coalminer* (2010) and

Nigel A Chapman's *South Staffordshire Coalfield* (2005). The local archives all have libraries of books, many out of print, and some local publications. It may be worth checking all the archives in the Black Country, as well as the William Salt Library in Stafford (www.staffordshire.gov.uk/leisure/archives/williamsalt/home.aspx), for relevant publications. There is an index to documents and publications held both at the William Salt Library and the Staffordshire Record Office, which is next door. A search on 'mining' in the online index on the William Salt website returns at least 1,000 records. Some of these relate to mining in Staffordshire but outside the Black Country, but there are many documents in the list that are relevant to the Black Country.

Chapter 3

INDUSTRIAL DIVERSITY

Introduction

By 1700 many metal-working trades were represented in towns such as Walsall. Here the largest group was probably the loriners, makers of saddler's ironmongery. Between 1650 and 1750 the population in Walsall trebled to accommodate the growth in industrial manufacturing. Typical operations were two-storey, backyard workshops, each with half a dozen or so workers. Other trades around the region included japanning and tinplate working in Wolverhampton, lock making in Willenhall, chain and nail making in Cradley Heath, glass in Stourbridge and domestic ironmongery and springs in West Bromwich. It is impossible to cover every facet of industry that was carried out in the Black Country, but a representative range is covered in this chapter. Resources to help with further research are also detailed.

Other Forms of Mining

In addition to coal and ironstone, other resources were mined in the Black Country, particularly limestone, which was mined extensively. The large seam of limestone in Dudley was used to build Dudley Castle and Priory. Dudley was one of the few castles mentioned in the Domesday Book: 'William is the tenant of Dudelei, his castle is here'. The stone walls date from the early twelfth century, while the walls of the hall within the castle were built from limestone rubble in the thirteenth century. Limestone was used extensively in the iron and steel industry as a flux in the smelting of iron. It was also used in making glass, being one of the three key ingredients in almost all commercially sold glass. Silica (sand) is the main component, along with soda ash and limestone, the latter rendering the glass less brittle; this mixture is then melted in a furnace at about 1700° C.

Limestone mining in Dudley peaked in the mid-nineteenth century, when 500,000 tons of limestone a year were extracted from the Wren's Nest Hill area, and despite this vast reserves remain there. It is possible

Wren's Nest Tunnel which shows a pillar of limestone. (With kind permission of Dr Trevor Raybould)

to visit the vast underground limestone caverns at Dudley on a boat trip, organised by Dudley Canal Trust; their site is a few hundred yards from the BCLM (see chapter 9). *Osborne's Guide to the Grand Junction, or Birmingham, Liverpool and Manchester Railway* (1838) noted a limestone mine: 'On looking round, you perceive a lofty roof 8 or 10 yards high, of apparently veined marble, sustained by massive and handsomely-formed pillars, at the distance of every 10–12 yards ... they have all the appearance of having been constructed'.

Clay was essential in the development of many industries in the region. It was used to make brick to line furnaces employed in iron and glass manufacture, as well as in more obvious processes. The discovery of large deposits of fireclay was one reason why the clay-making industry developed around Stourbridge. Clay was often found in the same mines as other mineral deposits. The Racecourse Colliery at the BCLM, which today it is set out as a coal mine, was originally mined for all four of its resources.

Reserves of glasshouse pot-clay existed around Stourbridge, especially in Amblecote in 1566, when a lease to dig for it was issued. Naturalist Dr Robert Plot said in 1686, 'the clay, which surpasses all others of this country, is that at Amblecot, on the banks of [the] Stour'. There is much evidence of the extraction of clay around Stourbridge in the late eighteenth century. Amblecote clay was ideal for making bricks and vessels for use in the furnaces in the glass industry.

Eventually, as clay mining developed, firebricks were supplied widely for use in furnaces across Britain and exported worldwide. Fine-quality fireclay lay beneath coal and ironstone reserves, and was also mined in Cradley Heath. It was also, on occasion, extracted using open-cast methods, for example, at the Marl Hole at Homer Hill called 'Spirit Hole'.

Glass Making

The history of glass making is a long one. About 400 years ago glass workers from Lorraine and Normandy were drawn to the Black Country because of the availability of coal and clay, which are necessary to make glass. Glass making developed and the Industrial Revolution saw advances in the industry and working practices. A very early mention of glass making is in church records at Kingswinford on 26 April 1612, when John, son of Paul and Bridget Tyzack, was baptised. The Tyzack name is a thread throughout the seventeenth century and beyond, and in more recent times Don Tyzack wrote an account of his family entitled *Glass, Tools and Tyzacks* (1995). Dud Dudley is also said to have smelted glass using coal on the Himley Estate, although he is better known as a pioneer in the iron smelting industry (see chapter 2).

The first glass houses in the district were cone-shaped. From the late nineteenth century onwards the design developed into the more traditional factory building, with a chimney instead of a cone. The light inside a glass house was quite dim, although there was plenty of glare from the metal in the pot (this floated to the surface of the glass mixture and had to be removed, leaving clear glass ready for working). Fireclay pots held the liquid, which was often coloured to suit the requirements of the piece being made. Chemical knowledge was necessary for successful glass making with oxides of cobalt and copper creating shades of blue, while iron produced green and yellow. The lehr (or lear), mentioned in the job description below, was an oven that was hot at one end and then, as glass progressed through it, became cooler, strengthening the glass in a process known as annealing.

Much of the best glass made in Stourbridge was cut crystal and an iron wheel was used to accomplish this. As the wheel spun water and sand dropped onto the edge, helping the wheel bite into the surface of the glass to produce the cut. A stone wheel then took away the roughness from the first cut and finally a wooden wheel gave a brilliant shine to the glass.

Between 1770 and 1930 there were about thirty glass factories listed between Dudley and Stourbridge, the main village centres being Wordsley, Amblecote and Wollaston, although the industry spread as far as Brierley Hill, Holly Hall and Dudley. One of the most famous glass-related landmarks still in existence is the Redhouse Cone at Wordsley. This dates from 1788 and is worth a visit if you have ancestors who worked in the industry (see chapter 9). It has been preserved and opened as a museum in 2002.

Many of the famous glass marques from Stourbridge have either disappeared or been swallowed up by multi-national corporations. Stuart Crystal, for example, the last operator of the Redhouse Cone, was taken over in 1995 by Waterford-Wedgewood and production was moved offshore in about 2001. Stuart produced much of the glass for the *Titanic* and some fine examples are on display at the Redhouse Cone. Thomas Webb and Sons was a successful glass house from its establishment by Thomas in 1854. His sons Thomas Wilkes and Charles continued the business when Thomas retired in 1863. In 1874 the great craftsmen Thomas Woodall joined the company. Woodall started cameo carving in glass about six years later. The best-known piece of carved cameo glass work is the ancient Roman Portland Vase on display at the British Museum in London; images and information about the vase can be found at: http://www.britishmuseum.org/explore/highlights/highlight_ objects/gr/t/the_portland_vase.aspx. In the late 1870s the Stourbridge glass maker Philip Pargeter made a replica of the vase which was then engraved by John Northwood. This vase won a £1,000 prize offered by local glass maker Benjamin Richardson. There is also a replica being made at the 2012 Stourbridge glass festival. In 1893 Thomas Webb and Sons displayed its work at the Chicago Exhibition, including high-quality cameo work, mainly by Thomas and his brother George Woodall. It attracted much attention, and this continues today. There is probably more British cameo glass in American collections than in Britain.

The definitive reference work for the glass-making industry in the Black Country is Jason Ellis's *Glassmakers of Stourbridge and Dudley 1612–2002* (2002). Another very useful guide is Graham Fisher MBE, *Jewels on the Cut* (2010), which makes the very clear link between the local glass industry and the Stourbridge Canal. For cameo glass see H Jack Haden's *Artists in Cameo Glass* (1993), which is available from the Black Country Society.

Broadfield House Glass Museum, situated in the historic Stourbridge glass quarter, has one of the best glass collections in the world. It includes objects that date from the seventeenth century to the present day and highlights the skills and creativity of glassmakers past and present. The museum is free to enter, has a gift shop and a hot glass studio and guided tours can also be booked. A very informative day can be spent at Broadfield House Museum and the nearby Redhouse Cone. To help the family historian, at Broadfield House there is a national index with names of many glass workers throughout history; the index is added to when new information comes to light. Researchers can also contact the museum for name searches to be carried out; for further information visit the website at: www.dudley.gov.uk/leisure-and-culture/museums–galleries/glass-museum.

Glass makers worked in teams of four, known as 'chairs', and their job descriptions are given in the table below.

Glass-making Jobs

Footmaker	Carried out initial gathering and blowing of glass
Servitor	Blew glass to form the basic shape
Gaffer or Workman	Most senior team member who carried out final hand-shaping of the piece
Taker-in	The junior member, who took the piece to the annealing oven or 'lehr' for cooling

The iconic Redhouse Cone, Wordsley, Stourbridge. (Author's photograph)

Some of the most famous names in British glass were located in Stourbridge. These include Thomas Webb, Stuart Crystal, Richardson and Webb, and Royal Brierley. Well-known individual artists working in the area included the Woodall Brothers, the Tyzack family, Frederick and George Carder, and John Northwood.

Chain and Nail Making

The Beach Report to Parliament, dated 1888, suggested that chain making started in Cradley Heath in about 1810. The chain industry owed much to Lloyd's Maritime Insurers as ships with iron cables were more secure than those with hemp rope. Children as young as 9 were taught to make chains and they practised on the iron branch that tied bundles of iron together.

Many women took jobs making chain as the work could be fitted in around looking after husbands and children at breakfast, household chores followed by the midday meal. In addition, there may have been pigs to feed, beer to brew, children to feed again and then the evening meal. Single women could work in factories throughout the day. In the 1830s, the peak of nail manufacturing in the Black Country, about 50,000 people were working in the industry. By 1883 16,000 of the 20,000 nail workers in the Black Country were women and children. Nail and chain making were skilled jobs and the larger items, principally chains, were produced in factories, for example Noah Hingley's (see below).

One of the iconic symbols of the chain-making industry in the Black Country is the anchor made for the *Titanic* produced by Hingley's. Much of the chain used in ship building was made in the region. The Round Oak Iron and Steel Works (see chapter 1), as part of its modernisation in the 1890s, set up a chain shop, and went on to make chain for use in the First World War. Chain was supplied to the Admiralty, and the largest chain in the world was made at Round Oak. This part of the business continued until the 1920s, when trade declined.

Noah Hingley was a pioneer in the making of chain and cable, and he established his business in 1820. By 1845 he had opened a large foundry and iron works in Netherton, and by the turn of the century the company was one of the country's leading chain makers. In addition, from 1850 Hingley's also began making anchors. As Hingley's business grew, the company expanded into coal mining in the Dudley Wood area, also extracting ironstone from the mines. Noah Hingley and Sons became a public company in 1890. Chains and anchors were sent around the country, especially to shipbuilders on Clydeside. As factory owners did not want to tie up space producing little items, smaller chain was made in a similar fashion to the nail trade using outworkers.

A copy of Kenneth Mallin's PhD thesis, 'Noah Hingley: The World's Premier Manufacturer of Ships' Anchors and Cables in the period 1890–1918' (University of Warwick, 1997), can be viewed at Dudley Archives. It deals with the first thirty years of the incorporated company, and while

A recently made replica of the Titanic anchor produced at Hingley's in Netherton, now on display in Netherton town centre. (Author's photograph)

The inside of a chain shop at the Black Country Living Museum. (Author's photograph, courtesy of the BCLM)

its scope is narrow, it is the only known competent account of the history of the firm. It has brief but useful sections on the firm's activities before 1890 and the main characters involved in its development.

There is evidence of nails being made in Britain in Roman times following the excavation of a Roman settlement site at Inchtuthil, Perthshire in 1960, with the site dated to about AD 85. By the fourteenth century a variety of iron nails were being made in Europe, and by the beginning of the sixteenth century Dudley was becoming known for its nails, some of which were used in the building of Nonesuch and Hampton Court palaces. In 1538 at Nonesuch nails were bought from Reynolde Warde, a nailman from Dudley, at the cost of 11s 4d per 1,000.

The Foley family were heavily involved in the nail trade. Richard was first, based in Dudley, and his son also Richard, known as 'fiddler Foley' (see chapter 1 for more on Richard Foley). Iron slitting, which made nail making much easier, was invented by the Swedes. Both Foley and Dud Dudley have been credited with some early industrial espionage by going to Sweden in the guise of a half-wit fiddler to gain access to a slitting mill. On Foley's return to Britain he unsuccessfully tried to duplicate the process. A second visit to Sweden revealed what Foley was doing wrong and at Kinver a slitting mill was established, laying the foundation of the great Foley fortune. Thomas Foley expanded the business and was able to purchase Witley Court, where he lived most of his life.

It was generally accepted that nail and chain makers were worse off than other workers such as miners. The average worker paid rent for his or her cottage and shop and had to find or make their own tools. If they had a small family they might let out stalls around the forge for 8d each per week. The iron to produce the nails was supplied by the nail master or merchant (often known as a 'fogger': the middleman in the nail and chain trade) in bundles weighing 60lb.

In 1860 Walter White came to stay with a Quaker friend in Birmingham. When he travelled to the Black Country he wrote of his experiences in *All Round the Wrekin* (2nd edn, 1860). He noted muddy canals, docks, mineral tramways, small trains, abandoned mine workings with great heaps of spoil as pit banks encroached over the grass and hedgerows. In Rowley he heard the thump, thump of hammers in almost every house; each cottage had a forge in place of a washhouse. In some houses there were three or four women hard at work, often assisted by a small boy or girl. The people were friendly and willing to talk. White said:

> the fire is in common and one after another giving a pull at the bellows each woman heats the end of two slender iron rods, withdraws the

first and by a few hammer strokes fashions and cuts off the nail, thrusts the end into the fire and takes out the second rod and gets a nail from that in the same way. The work goes merrily on.

One woman told White she used to be able to start work on Tuesday and make 13s a week, but the handmade trade was then in decline. This change was brought about by cheaper materials, imports of cut nails and mechanised processes.

Women were the mainstay of nail making in places like Cradley Heath, Halesowen and Lye Waste. It was exhausting work, up to 12 hours a day. The wage was paltry, between 2s 6d and 5s per week. These women lived in poor domestic circumstances and were pale and thin, with wiry and muscular arms. Their homes were not tidy, probably due to the hours they worked making nails or small chain. In some households they were the main bread winners, their idle husbands taking advantage of them. To get a picture of what life was like for nail makers, a contemporary account was written by David Christie Murray called *A Capful o' Nails* (1896), and this vividly describes conditions under the truck system. On the Sandwell Council website at: www.sandwell.gov.uk, enter 'chain making' in the search box and you will find plenty of resources and references on the subject.

Nail and chain makers were often subjected to corrupt practices by the fogger. In an effort to maximise profits they used underhand tactics, many at the expense of the nail maker. Workers would be underpaid, charged high rents for a forge, the weighing of the final product fiddled with and poor quality iron given out but disguised as best quality (see the image on p. 53). They would also use 'truck' tokens instead of paying for work in cash, and would lend money to workers when times were hard at exorbitant rates of interest.

At Dudley Magistrates on 26 April 1869 nail factor Samuel Woodall, of Flood Street, Dudley, also landlord of the Miners Arms of Market Place, Dudley, was charged with having a pair of unjust scales with an 8oz piece of lead attached. His defence was that it was to compensate for the slack and rubbish the nailers mixed with the nails. The prosecution stated that allowance was always made for this; they also alleged the altered scales had been in use for three years. Woodall was found guilty and fined the maximum of £5 and costs.

Around the turn of the twentieth century there was much political discussion of 'sweating' (a word used to describe home working such as nail making). In 1907 a House of Lords Committee defined the practice as involving unduly low rates of pay, excessive hours of labour and

PUBLIC APOLOGY.

Whereas I, Samuel Smith, Horsenail Maker, residing at Rowley Regis, near Dudley, have been detected in an attempt to defraud Messrs. SAMUEL EVERS & SONS, of Cradley Iron Works, by exchanging the Bands and re-bundling their "Second Best Rods," so as to make them imitate and appear like their "Charcoal Horsenail Rods," TO THE PREJUDICE & INJURY OF THE SAID SAMUEL EVERS & SONS; and they having consented (on my humbly begging their pardon, and making a public apology for the same), to forego prosecuting me.

Now I do hereby acknowledge the offence AND MAKE THIS PUBLIC APOLOGY, and sincerely thank them for the pardon so granted ME.

SAMUEL SMITH, his mark ✗

Witness SAMUEL LEONARD.

January 23d, 1843.

Nail-maker Samuel Smith's public apology for corrupt practice. (Author's collection)

insanitary conditions in the workplace. The area around Cradley Heath was a major centre for the practice. The reason many nail makers were women was that their husbands tended to have better paid jobs in factories and did not want to work from home for lower wages. In 1910 in Cradley Heath women were paid as little as 1*d* per hour. The government passed legislation to implement the first minimum wage to tackle this 'white slavery'. The workshop chain makers were then locked out of their rented workshops by their foggers. This led to a ten-week battle, involving Mary MacArthur, who garnered substantial public support through a well-publicised campaign. Eventually, the women won their battle and were paid the minimum wage. This action would lead to the demise of 'sweated' labour. A recent work on the women chain makers' struggle is Jean Debney's *Breaking the Chains* (2010).

Lucy Woodall – Last of the Women Chain Makers

In the early 1970s there was still one woman working as a chain maker in Cradley Heath – Lucy Woodall née Swingler, who had begun chain making almost sixty years before. For four mornings each week Lucy worked at her hearth at the factory of Samuel Woodhouse and Sons, in Corngreaves Road, where she had begun working in 1957. From 1959 she worked part-time and retired for two weeks in December 1969, commenting: 'I've always enjoyed my job – I've always been comfortable'. Her long years of chain making had given her physical strength and it was clear during an interview with Peter Barnsley for an article that appeared in the autumn 1971 issue of the *Blackcountryman* magazine that she was going to work for as long as possible. She was the last of the army of women chain makers to have worked in the Black Country.

Lucy Swingler was born in Old Hill in 1899 to a mother who was a nail maker. By the age of 13 Lucy was herself an apprentice chain maker, working 12-hour week days and 7 hours on a Saturday. She was paid 4s a week for the first six months, then her wage rose to 5s 6d. After twelve months Lucy moved onto 'stint' work, and once she had completed her allotted quota of work for her stint she would continue to work at piecework rates. When she was 15 she was only working piecework. In the twenty-first century Lucy's life seemed harsh, and her only holidays were in later life, visiting friends in Chipping Norton. In her youth time off was confined to day trips and 'holidays' picking hops at Callow End in Worcester (see chapter 6 for information on hop picking).

In 1927 Lucy married a collier, John Woodall, but he died after only four-and-a-half years of marriage; she remained a widow for the rest of her life. Lucy died in 1979 aged 80 and it is not known when she gave up work. She was a remarkable character, a throwback to an earlier age.

Early issues of the *Blackcountryman*, the magazine of the Black Country Society, contain articles on various aspects of nail making. In addition, two books by local author Ron Moss are also worth reading: *Chainmaking in the Black Country* (1995) and *Chain and Anchor Making in the Black Country* (2006).

There is a surviving chain shop at Mushroom Green in Cradley Heath. In 1871 William Kendrick was carrying on the trade of chain making here, and his son Harry took over on his death. Harry worked as a chain maker until 1961, when he was 76 years old; he died in 1965. In the 1970s

The chain shop at Mushroom Green, Cradley Heath. (Author's photograph)

the building they had occupied was in danger of being demolished but the Black Country Society was eventually given permission to restore it as a chain shop. In 1975 Mushroom Green was quoted as being 'the only outstanding conservation area in the West Midland County'. In June 1975 work commenced in earnest and was finished in February 1976. The chain shop opened for demonstrations on a regular basis for thirty years before closing for a time. It is now open again on certain dates, and for opening details visit the Industrial Heritage Stronghold website at: www.industrialheritagestronghold.co.uk.

Early Motor Industry

In 1826 Absolom Harper started a business making fenders at Waddam's Pool in Dudley. The business continued with his sons, John and Edward. John's only daughter married George Bean in 1879 and he joined the family business in 1884, becoming principal shareholder when the company was made limited in 1901.

By 1911 about 200 people were employed at 'The Bean', supplying forgings for the emerging motor industry. The company expanded during the First World War, making munitions. After the war the firm dramatic-ally changed its business to motor-vehicle production, planning to mass-produce cars similar to the Model T Ford. The chassis was built in Tipton and driven to Dudley for finishing. A model was produced, with a plan to build 10,000 a year. The first 'Bean' was unveiled in November 1919 at London's first post-war motor show. The first production model rolled off the line on 16 December 1919, registration number FD 1180. Output never achieved the dream as problems brought about by rising wages led to price increases and falling sales. Despite the fact that prices were cut in September 1920, a receiver had to be appointed and Tipton pro-duction ceased in October 1920.

'The Bean' returned to private ownership and new and re-vamped models were released, including commercial vehicles. However, in 1931 the company again went into receivership and one profitable arm of the business, Smethwick Drop Forgings, was floated off, acquired by Guest, Keen and Nettlefold (GKN). But the Bean name lived on. In 1956 Bean Industries was purchased by Standard Triumph and drawn into British Leyland in 1968. The legacy was about 17,500 cars and 6,400 commercial vehicles. There are two Bean vehicles, a car and a tipper truck, at the

A Bean 14 Tourer motor car, on display at the Black Country Living Museum. (Author's photograph, courtesy of the BCLM)

BCLM. There is a Bean Car Club, with a website at: http://back.to/bean, and a written history of the company by Jonathan Wood, *The Bean* (2001). Finally, deeds relating to Waddam's Pool Works are held at Dudley Archives.

Other Motor Manufacturers in the Black Country

Clyno	Originated in Northamptonshire, but the owners moved to Wolverhampton to be nearer to their engine producer and a skilled labour force. Clyno motorcycles were built from 1909 and cars from 1922. Sales were good, but shortage of capital caused liquidation in 1929
Guy	Leading commercial vehicle manufacturer, set up by Sidney Guy, ex-works manager at Sunbeam Motor Company. First to introduce six-wheeled pneumatic-tyre motor buses, and started making trolleybuses in 1926. Taken over by Jaguar in 1961, by 1978 production of the longest surviving name of all Wolverhampton-made motors came to an end
Villiers	Produced motorcycle engines used by a large number of manufacturers. Originally set up to make pedals for Sunbeam cycles, the company moved into engine production and developed the two-stroke engine. Villiers suffered from the decline of the British motorcycle industry and was taken over by the owners of Norton, AJS, Matchless and, later, Triumph. The company closed in the 1970s
AJS	Founded by four sons of Wednesfield blacksmith Joe Stevens. They were pioneers of the motorcycle trade and manufacturers of one of the most renowned marques of all times. By 1897 the first Stevens engine had been built and used in cars, boats and motorcycles. The AJS name was used for Stevens own motorcycles, using the initials of their brother Albert Jack. The company was sold in 1931 and moved from the Black Country
Star	Star was in continuous production from 1899 to 1932. Edward Lisle began building velocipedes in about 1869 and the Star Cycle Company made parts for the Bushbury Electric Cart in 1897 before the Star Motor Co. was established. By 1914 Star was one of the biggest motor manufacturers in Britain and made large numbers of cars and commercial vehicles during the First World War. Rapid development followed, but Star was taken over by Guy Motors in 1932 and closure followed
Sunbeam	Founded by John Marston in 1887, it became an illustrious name in the production of cycles, cars and motorcycles. The company also made commercial vehicles, aero engines, planes and the famous Seagull outboard engine. The Sunbeam motorcycle came into production in 1912, and over twenty-five years gained racing success and a worldwide reputation for quality

Leather Making and Loriny

Leather items existed in Egyptian times and the Greeks and Romans also made good use of leather. Leather tanning is known to have been carried out in Britain in early times and evidence of a tannery dating to about AD 200 has been discovered at Lullingstone Roman Villa in Kent. Most medieval villages had at least one leather worker, who was essential to the local economy.

Saddlery was one of the main leather industries and Walsall became one centre where it flourished. Before saddlery became such an important industry there was a well-established lorinery trade. Walsall developed as a leather manufacturing town because of the availability of animal hides, iron ore and limestone. Many businesses were small and employed eight to ten people, some skilled, others working as labourers. At the height of the trade there were eight tanneries in and around Walsall. The smell was terrible as the work was done in the open air and the smell lingered over the whole town. The industry declined in the 1930s due to foreign competition, but has recently revived, and now there are over sixty saddlers based in the town, but no tanneries. There are still tanneries in Britain and the nearest is probably in Northamptonshire.

In 1793 Jabez Cliff started business as the first major saddler in the Walsall. His 13-year-old son George began his apprenticeship preparing bridles in the same year. Jabez Cliff is still in existence today, led by the seventh generation of the Cliff family. The opening of the Walsall Canal in 1799 was the catalyst for Walsall's emergence as a leather centre. In 1801 there were 29 saddlers and harness makers and by 1841 this had increased to 141. The industry grew rapidly and in 1881 there were 3,492 saddlers and harness makers, together with 430 tanners and curriers. Numbers peaked in 1901 when a quarter of the national total of saddlers and harness makers were based in Walsall – 6,830. Unfortunately, there are few records of the workforce as it was highly mobile within the town.

Leather-making Jobs

Tanner	Took the hide, cut front (hair) and back (fat) away. The hide was first treated in a lime pit
Currier	Finished preparation of the hide
Manufacturer	Used hide to make the finished product

The Leather Museum in Walsall, which is well worth a visit if you have leather-making ancestors. (Author's photograph)

If you are interested in the leather industry one of the best sources of information is Walsall Leather Museum (see chapter 9). The museum, housed in an old leather factory, was opened in 1988 by HRH Princess Anne and houses many artefacts, examples of locally made saddles and displays of loriny. There is also a library at the museum, open by appointment only, which contains plenty of material on saddlery, a photographic archive (with many items named), a good selection of trade directories and 100 oral histories, some of which are transcribed.

Other resources of use in researching the leather industry include Michael Glasson's *Walsall Leather Industry: Saddlers to the World* (2003); Michael is also the curator at the Walsall Leather Museum. Walsall Local History Centre has a selection of works for sale on the industry, for example Ann French's *Thomas Newton: A Pioneer of the Walsall Leather Trade* (1995). If you are interested in learning more about loriners, visit the website of the Worshipful Company of Loriners at: www.loriner. co.uk/loriners/splash.asp. The company has existed since 1261 and has held a Royal Charter since 1711.

Brick Making

The best fireclay was found around Stourbridge, and is said to have derived from the Rowley Hills when attrition from the hills was deposited as silt. Then tropical rain forests, which once covered much of the Black Country, grew, died and formed coal on top of the fireclay layer. Before the Industrial Revolution clay from Amblecote was so good that it was transported as far as London, no mean feat given the lack of good transport routes.

There are early examples of local bricks being used in the Black Country. The clay for the bricks used to construct the steeple at the chapel of All Saints Church, Bloxwich in 1702 came from nearby Lee Hill. Until the 1970s one of the coping stones to the gates of Brierley Hill churchyard bore the inscription 'Wm Mees made this in 1765'. By the 1830s Staffordshire was second only to Lancashire in brick making. In 1834 the Black Country boasted forty-three brick works, twenty-one of which were located in the Sedgley/Kingswinford area. In 1840 129 million bricks were made. Some of these local companies included J Whitehouse of Bloomfield, which made blue bricks for canal towpaths and bridges, Barnetts of Tividale, Blades of Leabrook, Tibbington of Tipton and Boys of Walsall.

One of the oldest established brick works in the Black Country was Harris and Pearson. The company began life as Fireclay, Stourbridge, founded in 1739 at 'Old Works' in Amblecote. It was taken over by Peter Harris and George Pearson in about 1850 and expansion quickly followed. In 1870 a new works opened, increasing the area covered by the company from 6 to 9 acres. Other mines were bought and leased, and by 1903 mining rights extended to over 100 acres.

Clay was mined and first picked over by women to ensure the right quality for the product to be made, for example, glass-house pots needed the fewest impurities to prevent failures in the pot. Once picked the clay was deposited in mounds for about twelve months to 'weather', a process that allowed wind and rain to disintegrate the clay, which initially looked like rock. The clay then went into the mill house where huge wheels crushed it into powder. The fine powder was sieved according to purpose. The powder was then 'tempered' with water and taken to the stoves, where it was worked into the required shape. The shaped product was taken to the kilns where it was baked at intense heat. Harris and Pearson exported worldwide, and their products all bore the company stamp.

Harris and Pearson brick works' building. (Author's photograph)

The Harris and Pearson building was erected in 1888 and every brick used was made by the company. The works was adjacent to the Great Western Railway and had its own railway siding, while on the other side lay the Stourbridge Canal. Harris and Pearson made a wide range of quality products and while its strengths lay in those products, it failed to move with the times and new processes and products passed it by. The company was taken over in 1968 by the Dyson Group but traded under its own name until about 1980. Further information and documentation, including transcripts of interviews with former employees, relating to Harris and Pearson can be found at: www.edu.dudley.gov.uk/humanities/HandP/teachernotes.htm. The company works was restored in 2005 and is a magnificent example of a building from that era, but the recent financial downturn has badly affected its value.

Lock Making

Lock making began in the Willenhall, Bilston and Wolverhampton areas of the Black Country during the reign of Queen Elizabeth I. One of the biggest iron manufacturers in the area was Willenhall Furnaces, which would undoubtedly have supplied much of the wrought iron for the lock industry. It also owned coal mines which provided the fuel to make the iron. In the seventeenth century Wolverhampton was considered the centre for lock making, but by the mid-eighteenth century Willenhall had taken over. In 1760 it was believed that 100 of the town's 250 houses were inhabited by locksmiths. Many of these businesses would have been very small. A 'Master' of the period employed about five workers, and many of these may have set up on their own later. One of the earliest factories in the town was built in 1790. By 1855 there were 340 workshops, supplying both British and overseas markets. Well-known names in the town were Josiah Parkes and Yale. In 1868 American Linus Yale had invented the modern pin-tumbler lock, which was ideal for mass-production. Yale came to Willenhall in 1929 and bought out an established lock-making company.

Between the 1851 and 1861 censuses in Willenhall, the population of the parish increased by 45 per cent. By 1770 there were 290 locksmiths in the area and by 1855 the number had risen to 452, with the growth area being Willenhall. Locksmiths worked mainly from home, assisted by family members and apprentices, some starting work as young as 9. Figures show that on average each locksmith would employ up to 10 workers, with a total of about 4,500 working in the industry in 1855.

Working conditions were very harsh and many locksmiths were cruel towards apprentices, hours were long – 70-hour weeks were common, conditions cramped and food poor. Children as young as 7 were employed at the vice. The mortality rate was very high, with many dying from contracting tuberculosis, typhus and cholera – in 1849 200 died during a cholera epidemic (see chapter 5). Willenhall was given the nickname 'Humpshire' because many young apprentices developed deformed backs and twisted shoulders as a result of the nature of their work and the effect this had on their young and soft bones. There is a tale that public houses had holes cut into the walls behind the benches to receive the humps of the men who came for their pints. Apprentices, if they survived, came to the end of their apprenticeship at about 21 years of age – they had been a cheap form of labour for the locksmith.

By 1889 a Locksmiths' Union had been formed, and this campaigned for better pay and conditions. Another change came in the early years of the twentieth century with the move from workshops to factories, with the consequence that larger firms invested in better equipment, power-driven lathes, drills and polishers. For most of the twentieth century Willenhall dominated the British mass-produced lock-making market and by the late 1950s the area was responsible for 90 per cent of British locks, latches and keys.

There is a preserved locksmith's house at 54 New Road in Willenhall, managed by the BCLM. It is not generally open to the public but is available for group visits and there are also occasional open days; visit the BCLM website for details at: www.bclm.co.uk/lhhome.htm, or telephone: 01215 208054.

The house and workshops date from the 1840s. In 1851 the property was occupied by Job Clark, a bolt maker who employed twelve men: 'Clark, Job, stamper by new registered stamping machine, and round and flat bolt manufacturer, New Road' (*Melville's Directory*, 1851). In the early twentieth century the house and workshops belonged to Job Phillips. He rented the workshops to Richard Hodson & Son, Lockmakers. The company was founded in 1792 and in 1893 it was taken over by John Hodson, who paid £47 to his late mother's estate for the business, shop tools and effects. He continued to trade under the original name and operated from several addresses in the Willenhall area before moving to New Road. In 1903 John and his wife Sarah bought the house.

Hodson's produced two types of padlock that were sold all over the world, including Cuba, Ecuador and Russia, and to a lesser extent in Britain. The first type was a lighter lock, used for fixing crates to the decks of boats. The second type was the bar padlock, used for securing gates and cattle compounds and in prisons.

Much of the Hodson house has been accurately restored as a typical Victorian dwelling, with gas lighting and contemporary furniture. There is an unusual collection of locally made locks and keys. The workshops still contain the machinery to manufacture the handmade padlocks that were produced there, now a thing of the past. Most of the small workshops that were prevalent in the town have since disappeared, so the preservation of this one is of great importance.

Nuts, Bolts and Screws

Darlaston is another major industrial centre that grew during the Industrial Revolution. In the 1750s the town was well known as a centre for gunsmiths who supplied Birmingham gun makers with barrels, gunlocks and every other necessary piece of 'smallwork'. However, Darlaston was also the major centre for the manufacture of nuts, bolts and screws. In 1876 there were forty-six factories making nuts and bolts and a further six making screws located in the northern towns of the Black Country (Royal Commission, *Factories and Workshops*, 1876). Bilston Museum once housed an 'English Oliver', which was the first bolt-forming machine and was attributed to Thomas Oliver of Darlaston. It was claimed that Oliver was the originator of the bolt and nut industry in Britain.

Other Trades

As previously mentioned, it was said that if it wasn't made in the Black Country it probably wasn't made anywhere. There is a long list of trades that relied on the major industries in the area. A representative sample of these businesses is listed in the table below.

Black Country Industry

Trade	Location	Sample Company Details
Bicycles	Walsall	For example, the Vanguard (1896) by Lunt, Wakefield and Mountford
Boiler Makers	Cradley	The Cradley Boiler Co., founded 1877
Boot Protectors	Stourbridge	Booth Brothers, Brettell Lane, started 1894
Boots	Old Hill	James Billingham, from late 1870s
Brush Making	Walsall	Bradnack and Sons, in business for over 200 years and still in operation today
Buttons	Halesowen	Groves, still operating
Cookers	Coseley	From 1884, Cannon Industries, in the 1950s Cannon made Britain's best-selling cooker
Enamelware	Bilston	Bilston was famed for its enamelware
Japanning	Wolverhampton	Bantock House Museum has a good selection of japanned items (see chapter 9 for details). Benjamin Mander set up an early japanning company in the town in 1791
Motorcycle Sidecars	Walsall	Swallow, founded by William Lyons, who was behind the Jaguar marque
Paint and Varnish	Wolverhampton	From 1803 Manders in Wolverhampton, Britain's largest manufacturer of paints, printing ink and varnish
Pottery	Smethwick	Ruskin Pottery Works, Oldbury Road (1838–1935)
Roofing and Bridges	Darlaston	Rubery Owen, from 1884

Trade	Location	Sample Company Details
Rope	Walsall	John Hawley, started in 1837
Scales and Weighing Machines	West Bromwich	W & J Avery, Atlas Foundry
Soap	Tipton	Tipton Soap Factory
Spades and Shovels	Stourbridge	B Fiddian and Son, from 1894
Spring Making	West Bromwich	George Salter began making springs in Bilston, before moving to High Street in the early nineteenth century
Stainless Steel		Old Hall, in 1930 William Wiggin made the first stainless-steel teapot in the world
Wrought-steel Holloware	Cradley Heath, Stour Works	Ernest Stevens, 'Judge' brand, also Izon's and Kendricks in West Bromwich

More examples of trades can be found in Michael Glasson's *Made in Walsall – Town of 100 Trades* (2005) and Ray Shill's *Birmingham and the Black Country's Canalside Industries* (2006). Trade directories are another useful source for the origins and scope of Black Country industry. Some can be found in printed form at archives and certain libraries. A useful online archive is at: www.historicaldirectories.org, which features nation-wide directories especially for the 1850s, 1890s and 1910s, with some going back as far as 1805. There is a county map to help you to narrow down your search and a facility to search by year. Many directories are also available on CD-ROM from genealogy suppliers such as S&N Genealogy. There are two series that are particularly useful, *Kelly's Directory* and the *Post Office Directory*. In *Kelly's Directory* residents are listed and there are sections on major towns and surrounding villages, which detail the history of the area in a similar way to a gazetteer. There is information on main trades, chief land owners and even coverage dates of parish registers. Editions of *Kelly's Directory* from 1890 onwards contain more residents, sometimes listed in a section called the 'Court Directory'. Editions of the *Post Office Directory* in the 1900s give comprehensive listings for residents and tradespeople of an area. Other series, such as *Pigot's Directory*, begin in about 1820 and cover major professions, nobility, gentry, clergy, coach and carrier services, taverns and public houses in an area. Entries include name, trade and address. *Slater's Directory* tends to be larger and covers the period from the 1850s.

During the Industrial Revolution trade unions became more prevalent. Around the country 5,000 unions are known to have existed, although some for only a very short time, including many that represented Black Country workers. The first legal trade union was set up in 1824, the Steam Engine Makers Union. Since that date many unions and friendly societies have been formed, some amalgamated and others closed down. The most useful initial resource for researching trade unions is the Trade Union Ancestors website at: www.unionancestors.co.uk, which lists all known unions and shows how some of today's major unions came into being. There is also good advice on where to find union records, for example, Warwick University Modern Records Centre which can be accessed at the following website: www2.warwick.ac.uk/services/library/mrc/explorefurther/subject_guides/family_history.

Chapter 4

TRANSPORT

Introduction

Industrial development in the Black Country relied on good transport links, and the two main methods, other than roads, were canals and railways. Rights to build roads, canals and railways were given to the likes of the Earls of Dudley, Bradford and Dartmouth, as well as industrialists such as the Foley family. Great improvement rights were granted to build canals, roads and railways to support industrial development during the late eighteenth century.

The lack of a comprehensive road system passing through the Black Country kept it relatively isolated from other parts of the country. A system of turnpikes was introduced connecting towns in the Black Country to Birmingham and this is described below. The introduction and development of canals, railways, trams and buses is also discussed, and there is a brief account of flight. The competition between canal and railway operators, the eventual decline of the railway network and the increased use of roads are examined. There is also an account of one of the worst railway disasters in Britain, when the carriages of an excursion train broke away and ran into another train following it.

Roads

In 1555 the first Highways Act placed responsibility for road main-tenance on the parish through an Overseer of the Highways. This proved to be an ineffective way of maintaining and developing the roads. In 1663 a further Highways Act allowed tolls to be charged and many Turn-pike Acts were passed between 1663 and 1836; between 1700 and 1750 ten Acts a year were introduced covering different parts of the country. By 1821 some 18,000 miles of roads covered by Turnpike Trusts had been completed nationwide. From 1889 onwards local district councils took over responsibility for main roads. In the 1960s the first motorways began to appear, and the motorway network now totally rings the Black Country.

In the early eighteenth century the condition of roads in the Black Country was very poor, which was not acceptable given the need to export goods. There are examples of glass transport to the Severnside ports of Bewdley and Bridgnorth being slow, with theft and breakages commonplace. In 1745 road conditions had not improved much, and John Wesley wrote that his horse had stuck fast in a quagmire on the high road near Wednesbury. It was little wonder that industrialists of the day turned to newer methods of transport, for example, canals.

Improvements to the road infrastructure of the Black Country began with the May 1727 Turnpike Act, which enabled tolls to be charged on existing roads from Birmingham, through West Bromwich to Wednesbury and Bilston. As a result, the quality of roads was improved. A separate road was to be built from Wednesbury to Great Bridge, then to Dudley and finally Stourbridge. This linked the coal-producing areas to glass manufacturers in Stourbridge. In the same year the Dudley, Halesowen and Bromsgrove Trust was formed. From Stourbridge roads were constructed to Bewdley, Bromsgrove, Kidderminster and Wordsley. Further

Woodsetton toll house, now located at the Black Country Living Museum. It was probably built in 1845 when the Sedgley–Tividale turnpike road was built. (Author's photograph, courtesy of the BCLM)

improvements took place following the introduction of the Enclosure Acts in the 1770s. While pedestrians were able to travel on the turnpikes free of charge, others had to pay and there was resistance to this, in particular, when existing road sections were turned into turnpikes.

At the end of the eighteenth century the Post Office began national mail-coach services. The Black Country was served initially by the Birmingham to Liverpool and Bristol to Manchester services. Thomas Fletcher was responsible for ensuring coaches came through Walsall. In 1781 he built the George Hotel, which became the main coaching inn for the town until the railway station opened at Bescot in 1837, after which coach traffic declined. The hotel survived until 1934, when it was demolished. To assist in the development of his business, Fletcher built the road from Walsall to Stafford, by obtaining an Act of Parliament; he also caused the Birmingham Road to be straightened and widened. Coaches with names such as the *Red Rover* and the *Crown Prince* passed through the town. Similar services existed in Wolverhampton, Bilston and other Black Country towns. At the beginning of the nineteenth century Bilston was on the route of the mail coach that travelled on the old Irish route from London to Holyhead via Chester. At the time, the Bulls Head was Bilston's principal coaching inn.

Coaches were occasionally involved in accidents. WH Duignan, writing for the *Walsall Observer* (9 February 1878), reported that a coach carrying convicts had overturned. The coachman lost control of his horses and the coach collided with the carriage of the Sheriff's Officer, Mr Perks, and as a result three men were killed. The prisoners were housed for a short time in Walsall before continuing their journey in another coach.

Canals

James Brindley built the first canal in England, at Manchester, in 1750. The first canal in the Black Country was the Birmingham Canal, the first section being completed in 1769 and the first load of coal delivered from West Bromwich to Birmingham on 6 November 1769. The impact on trade was immediate and the coal price in Wednesbury fell from 13s to 7s a ton. The first canal that came near Dudley was James Brindley's Birmingham Union Canal, built in 1775, which passed Dudley at Tipton. The canal system grew quickly, with the Staffordshire and Worcester-shire Canal (1772), the Dudley and Stourbridge Canal (1778) and Dudley No. 2 Canal (1798).

One extraordinary feat of engineering was the 2-mile-long Dudley Canal Tunnel, which passes beneath Dudley. It is the second largest canal

A section of the Stourbridge Canal, near the Redhouse Cone. It is distinctive because there is a sunken concrete canal barge submerged on the bank, the front of which has two trees growing out of it. (Author's photograph)

tunnel in existence in the British canal network and was completed in 1792. It took seven years to build, four years longer than planned. A series of problems caused the delays: the original contractor, John Pinkerton, failed to keep to schedule; the engineer, Thomas Dadford, the only man on the project with significant experience of canal construction, was headhunted; sub-standard locks were built; and the project ran out of money and needed re-financing. Eventually, in October 1792, it was completed. Dudley Tunnel is a 'legging' tunnel, without a towpath and its entrance is a major attraction at the BCLM. See J Ian Langford's 'The Building of Dudley Canal Tunnel', in the guide *Dudley Tunnel* (1973), edited by Derek Gittings and published by the Dudley Canal Trust, which was produced to celebrate the reopening of the tunnel. The original papers relating to the tunnel's construction are in Dudley Archives.

In a 1794 Act of Parliament industries were authorised to construct their own branches to the main canal system. Some of these links remain today, or can at least be traced, while others have been lost. In the late

70

1790s Walsall was connected to the Birmingham Canal by the Birmingham and Wolverhampton Canal. This completed the initial group of canals that connected the main industrial towns of the Black Country. The canals carried passengers as well as freight and were transported by packet-boat services that ran several times each week. For example, in 1851 Swift Packets, run by Thomas Monk of Tipton, was carrying passengers from Wolverhampton to Birmingham via Tipton in 2 hours 10 minutes for 1s.

By the start of the nineteenth century the canal system was becoming overcrowded and inadequate. Thomas Telford was appointed to make improvements to the Birmingham Canal, which involved shortening and lowering the canal and removing some of its locks. Possibly the best example of this operation is the canal cutting at Smethwick. In the mid-nineteenth century work also began on the Netherton Tunnel and was finally completed in 1858. It was the widest canal tunnel in the country and was over 3,000yd long. Builders had learned the lessons of previous tunnels, making it wider with towpaths on both sides to reduce

Entrance to the Netherton Tunnel. (Author's photograph)

congestion. Initially, it was lit by gas and later had electric lighting. It was the last canal tunnel to be built in the Britain.

The decline in canal building began in about 1860, with the arrival and development of railways. However, canals continued to be the main form of transportation for the coal and iron trades for a number of years. This was unusual and came about because of the proximity of canals to the mines, foundries and works. It was the advent of cheap road traffic in the twentieth century that finally finished the canals, although the rail network did provide stiff competition for the roads.

Once canals were superseded by roads, many fell into disuse and became overgrown and filled with rubbish. Happily, through the efforts of British Waterways, Birmingham Canal Networks and other organisations, such as the Staffordshire and Worcestershire Canal Society, the canal network is now being given a new lease of life through leisure activities. The clean-up has also introduced bird and fish populations, including swans. An excellent way of seeing the aftermath of the Industrial Revolution is by canal narrow boat.

Netherton Canal during the annual canal festival. (Author's photograph)

Boatmen's Missions

The Incorporated Seamen and Boatmen's Friend Society was established in 1846 to improve the lives of men and women who worked on the water. The West Midlands area was unique as it was served solely by narrow canals yet had enough boatmen to warrant the building of permanent mission halls. There were five missions, run by the Incorporated Seamen and Boatmen's Friend Society, on the Birmingham Canal network in the Black Country, for example, at Top Lock, Walsall, which opened in 1901. The mission halls were often called 'coffee rooms' and provided refreshments, washing facilities, newspapers and games. One of the helpers would also take down letters on behalf of boatmen at no charge. It was hoped the facilities would keep boatmen out of public houses. At the Walsall rest four services were held each Sunday, one of which was Sunday school and 'children from the cabins' were welcomed. Missioners would also go out onto wharves, distribute hymn books and lead singing from the top of one of the cabins. In 1912 17,690 people visited the coffee rooms in the Black Country, 'mainly boatmen'.

The Society also took an interest in boat houses, and erected stables at strategic locations to accommodate horses when there were long delays for boats to pass a flight of locks. This was a bonus in winter. There were stables in the Black Country at Walsall, Ryders Green, Rushall and Great Bridge. The mission at Tipton was on Hurst Lane/Factory Road, and was built in 1892; much of the £1,000 building costs were donated by the Earl of Dudley.

Canal missionaries and chaplains made an important contribution to the social and moral welfare of boatmen. Wendy Freer and Gill Foster's *Canal Boatmen's Missions* (2004) provides more information about these missions.

Words and Phrases Used by Black Country Boatmen

Backerin'	Allowing a well-tried horse to make his own way along the towpath without a 'driver'
Boat Snapper	Workman in charge of boats in a basin. It was his job to keep them tied up, baled out and generally in a safe condition
Chuff Basket	Basket containing the boatman's food (chuff) usually hung from the horse's harness
Draw Level Hand	Term indicating both men working a boat were drawing equal pay. Normally, the captain took payment and then paid his helper

The New Cut	The Tame Valley Canal
The Test	The building at Factory Locks, Tipton, where boats were filled with weights and registered with their capacity
Tommy	Food, derived from 'Tommy Shops'
Travel Overland	Phrase used when boatmen had to travel with their horses by land to collect an empty boat. The horse dragged the tiller, the 'starn' (stern or steering lever) and the 'mast' (for connecting the tow rope to the boat)

Researching the Waterways

The Inland Waterways Association has a historical section that can be accessed at: www.waterways.org.uk. British Waterways has extensive archives and details of narrow-boat families, and information on how to access these can be found on its website at: http://britishwaterways. co.uk. The National Waterways Museum at Gloucester is also a useful resource (www.gloucesterquays.co.uk/content/nwm.php). More locally, the Staffordshire & Worcestershire Canal Society (www.swcanalsociety. co.uk) and the Birmingham Canal Navigations Society (www.bcn-society.co.uk) provide a great deal of background information. The London Canal Museum has an informative website at: www.canal museum.org.uk/collection/family-history.htm, which features oral accounts by boatmen and plenty of advice on researching boatmen ancestors.

A book that gives a flavour of the Black Country canal system, with maps showing the main features and locations of many canalside industries, is Michael Pearson's *Pearson's Canal Companion for the Stourport Ring: Black Country Canals* (2011). Many books have been written about Black Country canals, and the following are particularly worthy of mention: Ray Shill's *Birmingham and the Black Country's Canalside Industries* (2006), RH Davies' *Canal Crimes* (2010) and Sue Wilkes's *Tracing Your Canal Ancestors* (2011).

Railways

The rail industry began in the Black Country in the 1820s, principally through a company formed by James Foster, a Stourbridge ironmaster, and John Urpeth Rastrick, from Morpeth, Northumberland. Foster, Rastrick and Co. built a new foundry in Stourbridge, and it was here that the company's first steam locomotive, the *Agenoria*, was built. It was instantly recognisable by its very tall chimney and had its first run, in front of a huge crowd, on 29 June 1829 at Shutt End on Pensnett Chase. The spectators included the Earl of Bradford and JH Foley, MP for Droitwich. In the first trials the locomotive and four carriages reached 7½mph; with 20 carriages and 920 official passengers and 300 'hangers-on' the engine pulled 131 tons at a speed of 3½mph. *Agenoria* was used until 1865 to move coal from Pensnett Chase to Ashwood, where there was a forge – Greensforge. In 1885 it was donated to South Kensington Science Museum and now stands in the National Railway Museum at York.

While *Agenoria* was being constructed, an order for three further locomotives was received, to be shipped across the Atlantic. One of the engines that went to the USA, the *Stourbridge Lion*, is still in existence today and can be seen in the Smithsonian Institute, Washington. For further information on James Foster, Roy Peacock's *James Foster of Stourbridge (1786–1853)* (2006) contains a detailed account of Foster and Rastrick's work.

By 1837 the rail boom had spread across the country, and in this year the Grand Junction Railway opened, running between Birmingham and Warrington, crossing the eastern part of the Black Country. The first railway in West Bromwich also arrived in 1837, with a station at Newton Road. Tipton was very well served by both the railways and canals, and at one time there were seven passenger railway stations and six freight depots, a sign of the intense competition to provide railway services.

The railway competed directly with canals, which were also still expanding. In 1825, for example, it cost 20s a ton to transport iron by canal to Liverpool and Manchester. This soon dropped to 15s per ton as newer canals opened. However, by 1844 the Grand Junction Railway reduced the cost to 12s per ton to the same destination. The early advantage of canals being located close to foundries and factories was soon equalled by railway builders.

Rail development was not always popular with the public. In 1874 Messrs Ward and Sons proposed a rail link from their new Priestfield Furnaces to join the LNWR railway at Willenhall. Ward had been asked to build a footbridge over the line at one point, for the convenience of the public as the railway was going to pass over an existing footpath. The response from Ward's agent was that if the public wanted to use the footpath, they must scramble over the embankment! This comment was challenged and responded to by Ward: 'You must be aware that it is impossible to carry on collieries and works without occasional disturbance of the surface of footpaths and if unable to do so we may as well close our collieries'. The local Board of Health was challenged on behalf of the more than 20,000 residents to deal with the situation or resign. They responded by threatening to have all rails crossing footpaths in the parish taken up. In the end it is not clear whether the bridge was built, but it doesn't appear on the 1882 Ordnance Survey map, and the railway was re-built in 1899 by the new owners of the furnaces, Patent Shaft and Axeltree.

Britain's railways were nationalised in 1948. By this time there was more of a trend towards road transport, both for freight and passengers. In 1955 steam locomotives were replaced by diesel and electric power. Local passenger services dieselised in 1957 and from September 1962 London expresses were also dieselised.

Cuts in local rail services began in 1962, before Dr Beeching reviewed the rail network. The local service from Wolverhampton to Stourbridge was withdrawn in July 1962 as it was considered uneconomic. Local rail enthusiast Michael Hale remembers the last trains on the line. He went to the booking office at Princes End station, where the clerk was trying to hold back her tears as she feared she had lost her job. The motor car played a large part in the demise of this and many other rail services.

Dr Beeching's reforms had a large impact on the rail network in the Black Country. His view was: 'if it doesn't pay, close it down'. Dudley station closed to passengers in 1964 and in 1967 became a freight-liner terminal for container transport serving the West Midlands. Services grew in the first year from 113 to 550 trains per week. It remained profitable up to 1981, when recession made closure seem inevitable. This came as a shock as it was still a profitable terminal, more so because of the newly announced Enterprise Zone at Dudley. A compromise was reached to keep the terminal open until December 1983 by transferring some staff to Birmingham, as well as making further savings. It finally closed in September 1987. A late closure came in March 1993, with the freight line from Bescot (Walsall) to Stourbridge Junction being partially shut down. This removed the last line running through Dudley and came about despite protestations about the effect this would have on the local economy.

Locally, there are two places to visit to gain more information and a sense of the atmosphere of the railways: the Birmingham Rail Museum in Tyseley, Birmingham (www.vintagetrains.co.uk) and the Severn Valley Railway (www.svr.co.uk). Both run regular steam-train tours, although the Severn Valley trains are reduced in the winter months. Further afield is the National Rail Museum in York (www.nrm.org.uk), where the steam locomotive *Agenoria* is on display.

There are many records available to assist you in researching your railway ancestors and to find out more about the development of railways in the Black Country. Many photographs, plans and documents exist in the archives across the region. At Wolverhampton, for example, there are records relating to Acts and Orders, dating from 1846, concerning railways, such as the Shrewsbury and Birmingham Railway Act 1846, and items such as the minute books of the National Union of Railwaymen. The place to begin any search is at: www.blackcountryhistory.org. Another useful website is found at: www.railwaysarchive.co.uk, and this features a search facility for rail accidents and holds digital copies of many railway history documents. There is a guide to looking for railway worker records at TNA, and this can be viewed on the website at: www. nationalarchives.gov.uk/records/looking-for-person/railwayworker.htm. There is no unified name index for workers, and not all company records have survived. The GWR archive website at: www.greatwestern.org.uk

Hampton Loade station on the Severn Valley Railway. (Author's photograph)

is one example of a website that is part of the British and Irish web-ring of railway sites, where more historical information can be found. Finally, there is assistance on trade-union records at: www2.warwick.ac.uk/services/library/mrc/subject_guides/family_history/rail.

Many books and articles have been written about Black Country railways and many articles published in the *Blackcountryman* magazine. A recent book is Andrew Doherty's *The Black Country and South Staffordshire: A Line-by-line Journey Through the Region's Railway Stations Past and Present* (2009), which provides useful route plans for the whole of the Black Country. Di Drummond's *Tracing Your Railway Ancestors* (2010) contains a wealth of information. The Railway Ancestors Family History Society has a useful website at: www.railwayancestors.org.uk, and has a wide range of CD-ROMs for sale featuring railway staff databases and back issues of its journal. It also has a comprehensive list of British Railway Companies online. Many railway staff records are available at Ancestry, including companies that operated in the Black Country. The records currently cover the period 1833–1963 and the database includes indexed images of employment-related records from a number of historic railway companies in England, Scotland and Wales.

Rail Accidents

The advent of the railway network also introduced some risks for those using it. The worst accident recorded in the Black Country was on 23 August 1858, when fourteen people were killed and many more injured. In fact, it was the only rail accident to result in loss of life in the Black Country until 1969, when two people died and thirty were injured at Monmore Green, Wolverhampton, when a passenger train collided with a freight train.

The 1858 accident took place between Round Oak and Brettel Lane stations, run by the Oxford, Worcester and Wolverhampton Railway (known colloquially as the 'Old, Worse and Worse'). The train was hired to take teachers and children on a Sunday school excursion to Worcester. The outward bound journey was completed safely, the train making a number of stops to pick up further passengers. By the time it reached Worcester there were 2,000 passengers in 45 coaches. For the return journey the train was divided into 2, the first train pulling 28 coaches, the second only 16. The first train reached Round Oak station at 8.10pm. In the official Board of Trade Accident Report, by Captain HW Tyler, it was noted that what happened next was: 'Decidedly the worst railway accident that has ever occurred in this country'. Tyler continued:

Shortly after it arrived at this station [Round Oak], the couplings gave way near the middle of the train, and 17 carriages containing about 450 passengers, with a break [*sic*] van behind them, began to run back down the incline towards Brettel Lane. A second train, also full of excursionists was following the first one, with an interval of 11 or 12 minutes between them; and the loose carriages ran back upon the second train with great violence.

As a consequence of this 14 died, 50 were severely injured and a further 170 applied for compensation for injury or damage to their clothes. At the Coroner's Inquest the guard in the brake van, Frederick Cook, had a verdict of 'manslaughter' returned against him and was committed to Stafford Assizes. Cook had given evidence that he had applied his brake early in the descent, and had jumped from the van just before the collision. The driver of the second train saw the van coming back towards him and slowed his train almost to a halt. An examination of the brake screw showed it had not been applied prior to the collision but had bent during the collision, meaning it could not have been tampered with afterwards. This was against the evidence given at the inquest by Cook. Captain Tyler criticised the rail company for the trust they had put in Cook: 'who proved to be anything but trustworthy and careful, and who, in not performing that duty with the attention that it required, caused the fracture of a defective coupling, and permitted the greater part of his train to run backwards down a steep gradient, on which it came into violent collision with a following train'. During the inquest there was evidence that couplings on the train had been repaired during the journey, but that Cook had apparently not carefully applied his brake as the train approached Round Oak, to stop carriages running forward onto the engine, rebounding and fracturing the couplings. Newspaper reports and the Board of Trade accident report can be accessed at: www. 84f.com/phome.html. As has been mentioned previously, the contemporaneous newspaper reports are both comprehensive and presented in a factual manner, although the inquest may not have taken proper account of all the evidence.

Cook was remanded in custody awaiting his trial. The judge, Mr Baron Bramwell, immediately dismissed much of the evidence as 'rubbish', and observed that the guard may have been treated as a scapegoat. After the jury had heard the judge's opening remarks they considered the matter and found that there was 'no true bill' against Cook for manslaughter. The prosecution offered no evidence and Cook was acquitted.

Trams and Trolleybuses

There is a difference between trams and trolleybuses. Early trams were horse drawn, then steam-powered, but the first trams that were truly viable and affordable were electric-powered. Trolleybuses did not require tracks in the road to run on. They had rubber tyres, but their power still came from overhead lines.

In 1855 the world's first tram system was introduced in Paris. This was followed in 1860 by the first in Britain at Birkenhead. The first Black Country horse-drawn tramways ran between Handsworth and Dudley Port, and in Wolverhampton, operated by Wolverhampton Tramways Company. The development of tramways in the Black Country was carried out by private companies, authorised under the Tramway Act of 1870.

In the early 1880s steam power quickly replaced horse-drawn trams. In 1881 the first steam tram went from Queen Square, Wolverhampton to Tettenhall. There were many advances between 1883 and 1886, and in less than a decade electric trams began to appear. The first line to be electrified was between Wednesbury and Bloxwich in early 1893. Other towns quickly followed suit by electrifying their lines, except Wolverhampton, which used embedded road studs to power its trams. By 1910 the Black Country had the largest narrow-gauge electric tramway system in Britain. The next stage of development was the advent of the trolleybus. In 1923 Wolverhampton had trolleybuses with rubber-tyred wheels, and by the 1930s trolleybuses had replaced trams across the region.

The early development of tram systems was somewhat chaotic, and tramway companies had to negotiate separately with local authorities. However, in the early years of the twentieth century a clear pattern of organisation was established. The co-ordinating committee was the Birmingham and Midland Joint Tramways Committee, which supervised day-to-day operations. Eventually, all drivers and conductors wore 'BMT' uniforms and there was interchange of tram cars and tickets. This form of organisation was to influence the development of bus services, which eventually replaced trolleybuses across the region.

By 1910 the route system in the Black Country was fully established. It was not as extensive as modern-day bus services, but the frequency of trams was as good as buses, though they moved more slowly at an average of 5–10mph. The tram system also offered goods and parcel services. The benefits for the Black Country of such a wide-ranging net-work included a greater choice of places for people to work and a larger population area for employers to draw their workforces from.

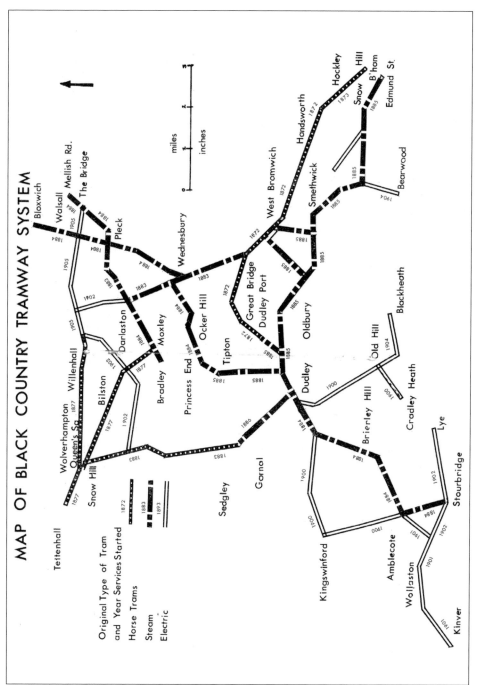

MAP OF BLACK COUNTRY TRAMWAY SYSTEM

Original Type of Tram
and Year Services Started

Horse Trams
Steam
Electric

Map of the Black Country tramway system. (Blackcountryman magazine, Winter 1972)

A Wolverhampton District tram, built in 1919, operating at the Black Country Living Museum in more recent times. (Author's photograph, courtesy of the BCLM)

Trams were also used for leisure purposes. The Kinver Tram, for example, ran from the Fish Inn at Wordsley to Kinver between 1901 and 1930. It carried thousands of people, especially on bank holidays. Trams were also used to take people coursing and dog racing, and pigeon fliers used trams to transport their pigeons on training runs.

In the years after the First World War trams began to decline. During the war track and tram repairs were neglected due to a shortage of staff, while the motor bus was also developing quickly. In addition, people were moving away from old-established town centres and main tram routes. Many of the Black Country tramways ceased operating between 1926 and 1930, and the last lines operated at Leamore and Bloxwich in 1933. The Midland Metro is a modern version of the tram system. From the mid-1980s a number of schemes were proposed for a tram system between parts of Birmingham and into the Black Country. Eventually, work began on the Metro in late 1995. The line runs from Snow Hill in Birmingham, through West Bromwich, into Wolverhampton. It opened in 1999 and since then passenger numbers have plateaued at about 5 million a year. The line is 12½ miles long and for most of its route follows the old Great Western Railway line between the two cities. Plans to extend the service with new lines and stations have so far not materialised.

There are many publications that focus on the tram era in the Black Country, including David Harvey's books, *Walsall Trolleybuses (1931–1970)* (2009) and *City to the Black Country: A Nostalgic Journey by Bus and Tram* (2009). Many of the photographic collections covering the Black Country feature trams and trolleybuses, as these were popular subjects for photographers.

Flight

The Midland Aero Club, one of the oldest private flying clubs in the country, was founded on 3 September 1909. It held its first flying displays at Dunstall Park in Wolverhampton. Its first official event was the inaugural All-British Flying Meeting, held in June 1910.

In June 1933 Wolverhampton Council set aside 178 acres at Barnhurst Farm (Pendeford) for a town airport. The land took two years to drain, having previously been used for sewage purposes. At this time Walsall and Birmingham were both going ahead with similar plans. Pendeford Airport opened in June 1938 at a cost of £80,000. The field was managed by the Midland Aero Club and until the start of the Second World War it was used by the nearby Boulton and Paul aircraft factory and private fliers. No scheduled flights came to the airport, much to the disappointment of Wolverhampton Council.

In 1939 the airport was requisitioned by the Air Ministry and became a training station. At the end of the war the future of the airfield was in doubt. However, the RAF still had a Flying Training School on the site, so it could not be closed. Elmdon (now Birmingham) Airport had become the main facility in the region, and Wolverhampton could only exist as a support facility. Details of RAF bases in the Black Country during the Second World War can be found in Appendix 1 at the end of this book.

In 1953 Don Everall Aviation Ltd and Wolverhampton Aviation Ltd applied for scheduled air services from Pendeford. Services to the Isle of Man, Derby, Jersey and Birmingham were established. However, there were no customs facilities and only a grass runway, which limited the scope for development. The 1950s did see a number of flying displays, including the King's Cup Air Race of 1950, as well as Goodyear Trophy races.

From the late 1950s there was growing opposition to the airport. The lack of facilities as well as new housing and industrial development around the airport were used as arguments against expansion at Pendeford. To counter this, Don Everall was doing a good job promoting the airfield. It had a fleet of Dakota aeroplanes, and ran one of the busiest flying clubs in the country, putting on regular displays for the public. In 1966 over fifty companies from ninety-seven other airfields landed planes at Pendeford.

A small, but significant, number of accidents marred the future of Pendeford. There were a number of training flight crashes in the Second World War. However, in April 1970 a twelve-seater De Havilland Dove crashed into a council house in Redhurst Drive, Fordhouses, killing an occupant in the house and the two-man crew of the plane. The airfield eventually closed at the end of 1970. Information on the history of Pendeford can be accessed at: www.localhistory.scit.wlv.ac.uk/articles/Pendeford/Pendeford.htm.

In the 1920s aeroplanes were using Calderfields in Walsall and on 6 July 1935 Walsall Airport, on Aldridge Road, officially opened. It was used by South Staffs Aero Club during its existence, but finally closed in 1957. There is archive material relating to both the aero club and aerodrome at Walsall Local History Centre and Alec Brew's *Black Country Transport: Aviation* (1994) contains further details.

The RAF Museum Cosford, at Shifnal in Shropshire, features exhibitions on the Cold War, an RAF timeline, airliners and RAF transport planes, war planes and some of the most exotic aircraft ever made. The RAF Museum in London has an extensive archive and many documents and artefacts are catalogued in an online database called 'Navigator'. For details visit the websites at: www.rafmuseum.org.uk/londonand www.rafmuseum.org.uk/cosford.

Chapter 5

BLACK COUNTRY LIFE

Introduction

Having examined the rise of the Black Country during the Industrial Revolution, and highlighted the main industries that emerged, prospered and waned, it is important to look at the people who lived and worked in the region. In this chapter a variety of subjects will be discussed, including the growth of the population, from the earliest time to the twentieth century; housing and living conditions; medical facilities and their development; education; dialect; and food and drink.

Local newspapers, reports of the Medical Officer of Health and council minutes and reports are useful sources of information, and these can all be accessed at local archives. Personal memories, diaries and visitors' accounts of the Black Country, often found in local archives and libraries, can also shed light on living conditions. These assist in creating a picture of what life was like for ancestors in different circumstances.

Population Change

Before the Industrial Revolution the Black Country was largely a rural backwater, untouched and undeveloped by outside influences. In 1086, in the Domesday Book, the area around Dudley was described as a poor, thinly populated area, with much woodland. The building of Dudley Castle and Priory, together with priories at Sandwell and Halesowen, had an impact on the southern part of the Black Country and subsequently on the growth of the population. The organisation of the priory and associated farming would have drawn people to the region. Wolverhampton developed earlier, from about 985. Walsall's early history is more difficult to chart. The first notable mention was in 1159, when King Henry II granted the manor of Walsall to Herbert le Rous.

Immigration into the Black Country came as a result of the increased need for workers. In the 1840s, Irish families were pushed east into England because of the Potato Famine and many settled in the Stafford Street and Caribee Island areas of Wolverhampton. Later, towards the end of the eighteenth century, more Irish came to work in and around the town on canals and railways, and they settled, perhaps because there was already an established Catholic population in the town. Miners came into the region from, for example, Derbyshire, Shropshire and Wales. The area of Darby End, just outside Netherton, is so named because of the Derbyshire influence.

The following table lists population figures for the Black Country over the nineteenth century. These figures show just how rapid population growth was in the Black Country, reflecting the emergence and development of the Industrial Revolution. As will be shown in this chapter, there was significant immigration to facilitate this growth, and merely relying on childbirth, especially given the living conditions in the region, could not have produced the numbers that are given below.

Black Country Population Figures

	Dudley	Wolverhampton	Walsall	West Bromwich	Stourbridge
1801	29,288	29,202	16,761	16,621	18,496
1811	41,243	38,206	18,900	20,557	22,244
1821	53,014	46,037	20,430	25,370	27,317
1831	66,396	58,125	24,926	35,183	34,984
1841	86,053	80,721	34,253	52,578	47,929
1851	106,530	104,158	43,044	69,729	57,350
1861	N/A	N/A	N/A	N/A	N/A
1871	134,125	136,053	71,834	106,626	73,386
1881	140,224	145,470	84,107	126,163	79,596
1891	142,705	154,864	100,112	142,584	82,824
1901	152,127	172,743	118,607	172,189	92,482

Figures taken from: www.visionofbritain.org.uk, using data tables for Poor Law Union/ Registration District

Emigration also occurred from the Black Country. The skills acquired during the Industrial Revolution made Black Country workers attractive to industries in other places. One of the most celebrated examples was the emigration of local people to Nanaimo, on Vancouver Island in British Columbia. In 1854 the Hudson Bay Company decided to recruit skilled miners from Britain. They engaged a Shropshire man, whose name is not known, to recruit twenty colliers and their families and transport them to Vancouver Island. A total of eighty-three people set sail on 3 June 1854. The voyage was a terrible experience, and one man, one woman and four infants perished on board. Those who did land safely remained in Nanaimo, providing a link between Canada and the Black Country. In 1954 Nanaimo commemorated the centenary of the landing of the miners and a representative from Nanaimo came to Brierley Hill to celebrate the occasion.

Dialect

A dialect is more than an accent but it is not a separate language, although it may have differences from the 'high' language. If you examine the Black Country and Birmingham, for example, those with a Brummie 'twang' are speaking with a different accent, not a dialect. Birmingham had more contact in formative years with outside influences and so its speech developed in conjunction with other parts of Britain.

Much research has been, and still is being, carried out into the Black Country dialect. As described earlier in the book, the Black Country was in a peculiar position during its formative years. Many people in the Black Country were isolated in small hamlets; there was poor literacy and no standard language for the written word; and those who could write were clerics who used Latin. From the fifth century onwards the dialect is of Anglo-Saxon and Low Germanic origins. After the Norman Conquest French was the language of the ruling classes and Anglo-Saxon the language of the majority. Those who lived in hamlets in the Black Country had no need to travel, even within their small community, as enough work was available to them there. During the Industrial Revolution there was greater immigration and also increased contact between other Black Country people. The dialect absorbed influences from elsewhere, and probably more importantly, people living in small settlements began to realise they were part of a greater Black Country.

Outside influences began to impact on the dialect with soldiers returning from foreign conflicts and people travelling through the region as trade routes opened up and transport links developed. This coincided with an increase in industry, with iron, for example, being made and then sold on outside the region.

An article written many years ago by William Henry Hensman (under the nom de plume Tom Brown), a well-respected Black Country teacher for forty years, compared the Black Country dialect with the language in Geoffrey Chaucer's *Canterbury Tales*. The article was published in an anthology on Lye and Wollescote compiled by Wesley Perrins MBE, but is not widely available now. Hensman found nearly 600 similarities in the way Chaucer formed his 'plural present', which matched the dialect habit of adding 'en' to the singular present tense of a verb. Examples of these corresponding words are 'they knowen' for 'they know', 'afeared' for 'afraid', 'fer' for 'far' and 'loff' for 'laugh'. Ed Conduit, author of *The Black Country Dialect* (2010), disagrees with this analysis, instead comparing the dialect with Old English, a Germanic language. Conduit does concur regarding the lack of Norse influence and cites the fact that there are many Anglo-Saxon place names in South Staffordshire and North Worcestershire, for example 'Seglesei' (Sedgley) and 'Ruh Leah' (Rowley, meaning broad and rugged land).

The future of the Black Country dialect is currently being examined, and it is thought that its linguistic identity is probably stronger now than it was during the period of the Industrial Revolution. Also, the dialect has survived the agglomeration of the Black Country into the wider West Midlands – it is believed that no one can take your dialect away from you. Another train of thought centres on 'tiers of protection', which breaks down into regional, local and micro aspects and then is ranked by trade and again within a trade. An example of this is that nailers spoke a particular dialect, 'nail-speak', and now that there are no nailers left this particular facet has died out.

There is plenty of written material available on this fascinating subject. Kenneth Malin's *Black Country: The Legend and the Myth* can be found in the reference section at Stourbridge Library. The *Blackcountryman* also has many references and examples of dialect, together with articles. Back issues of this magazine are still available in printed form or on CD-ROM, and indexes of these can be accessed via the Black Country Society website at: www.blackcountrysociety.co.uk. There are also relevant books available from the Black Country Society, such as Kate Fletcher's translations of the Old Testament and the Gospels into 'Black Country'. Another useful website, www.sedgleymanor.com, has a dictionary section that includes many Black Country words.

Samples of Black Country Dialect Words and Sayings and their Meanings

Afeard	Afraid
Baisn't	Isn't
Bibble	Pebble
I bin	I am
Bist	Are you
Blart	Cry
Bostin'	Great, very good
Chobble	Chew

Clammed/clemmed	Hungry
Cor	Can't
Dai'	Didn't
Doh	Don't
Ferkle	Mess about with
Fittle	Food
Fode	Yard or alley
Fust	First
Gawp	Stare at
Ginnel	Entry between houses
Gizz a goo	Let me try
Gooen	Going
Hotch up	Move over
Kayp owt th'ossrowd	Stay on the pavement
Lomp or Thrape	Beat or thrash
Lezzer	Pasture or field
Loose	To let go
'Ommer	Hammer
Ow bin yer?	How are you?
Podge	Jump a queue
Puddin' bag	Cul-de-sac
Reechy or Riffy	Dirty
Suck	Sweets
Summat	Something
Tay	Tea
Ter goo	To go
Wammel	Animal
Yo' con	You can
Yampy	Deranged or mad
Yo'm saft	You're silly

The material in this table is merely a small sample of words and no account has been taken of where in the Black Country these words and phrases originated.

Housing, Sanitation and Facilities

The expansion in population in the Black Country during the Industrial Revolution transformed the region into a densely populated conurbation around the main towns of Dudley, West Bromwich, Wolverhampton and Walsall. In Lye in 1820, 'There was not one house in fifty that was not built of mud and thatch', but from about 1850 brick-built houses began to replace the mud cottages. During the 1840s the conditions many people lived in were very poor. Housing provision did not keep pace with population increases.

In 1876 a programme of slum clearance took place in Walsall. Dr James MacLachlan, the first Medical Officer for Walsall, pointed out a number of streets that needed to be cleared. Included in his list were Town's-end Bank, Stafford Street, Green Lane, Wolverhampton Street and Marsh Lane. A total of 120 dwellings were compulsorily purchased, with a view to redevelopment, providing proper sanitary arrangements, such as light and air to two sides of each building; thorough ventilation; and a supply of water and a separate closet. The number of residents displaced was 592, but the replacement housing was for a minimum of 343. The final recommendation was that no occupation should take place until the roads had efficient sewers and paving (Royal Commission, Housing of the Working Classes 1884–1885) (1885). The area redeveloped in Walsall has since been altered again, possibly a number of times. A similar situation existed in other towns, and in 1875 Joseph Stokes, the Mayor of Dudley, issued a request for support with slum clearance. In Wolverhampton conditions were also poor, and once again houses were built too closely together and sanitation was inferior.

Residents also had other problems to cope with, for example, subsidence and the collapse of houses as a result of the amount of mining that took place, in particular around Dudley. It seemed that mining took precedence over housing. The pub nicknamed the 'Crooked House' (the Glynne Arms) on Himley Road is situated above a coal mine. It is now a local landmark as the building tilts some 15 degrees and so if a coin is rolled along the bar, it appears to move uphill.

The BCLM has a selection of houses that show how previous generations lived. One unusual exhibit is a pair of iron houses, built in the 1920s and originally located on Birmingham New Road, Dudley. There were about 500 of these built across the country, but only four in the Black Country. They were not a great success as they were more expensive to build than traditional brick houses, although they did make use of spare foundry capacity. Maps of the area are valuable resources in trying to find out more about where an ancestor lived. Through studying these it is possible to track the changes in a particular area over time. The best place to locate collections of maps is the relevant archive in a particular area. A good source of reproduction maps are Alan Godfrey Maps and Cassini.

The pair of iron house, originally located on Birmingham New Road, Dudley, and now at the Black Country Living Museum. (Author's photograph, courtesy of the BCLM)

Trade directories can give a flavour of an ancestor's life. The first of these was produced in 1677 and comprised a list of London merchants. Directories covering Staffordshire and Worcestershire include *Pigot's*, *Slater's* and *Kelly's*. Certain issues of these can be found in local archives and some libraries, and are also available on CD-ROM from the likes of S&N Genealogy. They are a selective resource, but help in establishing what commerce was present in a town at a given time. Many directories are also available online at: www.historicaldirectories.org/hd/. The Black Country directory *Jones's 1865 Mercantile Directory of The Iron District of South Staffordshire and East Worcestershire* is available to purchase on CD-ROM online at: www.parishchest.com.

Medical Problems and Facilities

Disease
In 1841 J Biddle, a surgeon resident for over twenty years in Willenhall, commented: 'Besides the numerous dirt-heaps, small pools and doorway slushes fronting or adjoining the dwellings and workshops, there are in

91

the town of Willenhall two vast masses of stagnant filth and putrescence, sufficient to breed a plague throughout the whole of England'. Shortages of clean water affected the whole of the Black Country, and in areas of digging carried out for railway cuttings and sewage removal local springs had drained of water. People were reduced to using water from pit workings and canals. Cholera was rife and in 1849 the disease killed 745 out of a total population of 20,000 in Bilston.

From the late eighteenth century 'Improvement Commissioners' began to be appointed in many towns across the Black Country. Wolverhampton was the first town to introduce them in 1778; Dudley had Town Commissioners in 1791; Walsall in 1824; and West Bromwich in 1854. In 1848 the Improvement Commissioners in Walsall laid down a sewerage system for the centre of the town. However, this did not solve the problem as the system was not capable of dealing with the sewerage created by pig-keeping and slaughterhouses. In 1871, Dr James MacLachlan commented on the health of Walsall, which he found to be 'tolerably good'. He pointed out that drainage, water supply and other sanitary arrangements were poor. In some places only one convenience was available for ten to twelve families. Incredibly, he also noted: 'In the kitchen of one [dwelling], in which there were a number of people and in which the cooking had to be done, I found a corpse' – and this was not the first time he had encountered this situation. As a consequence Dr MacLachlan recommended the establishment of a public mortuary; this account is based on reports in the *Walsall Free Press*, 7/10/1871.

Cholera was not the only disease causing problems in the Black Country. Smallpox was also prevalent, and an epidemic in Quarry Bank in 1894 caused great concern to the villagers. This outbreak was unusual because a vaccine had been developed by Edward Jenner in 1796, and administration of it was compulsory from 1853. The problem the Quarry Bank Local Board faced was the lack of isolation facilities. The advice of the Medical Officer, Dr Tibbetts of Cradley Heath, was that cases should be isolated, but there was no nearby hospital, so Army tents were hired for the purpose. These were sited at Merry Hill, in a field well away from the village. When fresh cases were diagnosed a horse-drawn cab would quickly arrive and the patient was taken to Merry Hill. Quarry Bank was not alone in the fight against smallpox. In 1893, 4,945 cases were reported in an epidemic in Walsall, with many victims having previously been resident in the area that had been the subject of the slum clearance in 1876. A total of 83 died, over 50 of whom were children. Walsall's medical services were under intense pressure; four trained nurses were engaged and hospital accommodation increased from 40 to 100 beds. A large heated marquee was also erected to serve as a children's ward.

Medication and Care

Before the general availability of doctors and hospitals, with access to drugs and the equipment necessary to diagnose and treat patients, people had to resort to other methods to cure their ailments. The provision of doctors in the Black Country is not well documented, but trade directories give clues as to the general availability. *Pigot's Directory* for Worcestershire in 1828, for example, lists 11 surgeons, 4 'chymists or druggists' in Dudley and 4 'chymists and druggists' in Stourbridge, along with 9 surgeons.

Many people used folk remedies, passed down from generation to generation. Some of these were specific to a locality and the Black Country was no different to other areas in this respect. Herb teas were very popular: broom to purify the blood, watercress for whooping cough and parsley for kidney problems. It is still common today to rub dock leaves on nettle stings to soothe the affected area, and usually the two plants grow together so dock leaves are readily available when needed. Other remedies were based on more irrational traditions: passing a child

A list of surgeons from Pigot's Directory, *1828.* (Author's collection)

> **SURGEONS.**
> Downing and Causer, High st
> Evans & Shipton, High st
> Freer William Henry, High st
> Hawkins Robert, Brierley hill
> Kitelee Ths. Hales Owen st, Oldby
> Nock John, Birmingham st, Oldbury
> Norris William, High st
> Perry John, High st
> Silvester Thos. Church st, Oldbury
> **TAILORS & MEN'S MERCERS.**

through a growing tree was thought to cure whooping cough, while inhaling the fumes from road tar was thought to cure a cold. This particular tradition is still well known today, probably for good reason. A less plausible remedy was described by John Freeman in his book *Black Country Stories and Sketches* (1930):

> *If you rub a golden ring*
> *Upon a powke* nine times*
> *The powke will surely go*

* 'powke' is the Black Country name for a stye on the eye.

Quackery was also common in the Black Country, and markets across the region often included stalls selling products that claimed to cure a variety of ailments. Walter White gives an account of Walsall market in *All Around the Wrekin* (1860). In one part he describes seeing a dozen stalls exhibiting an array of jars and by each stall there is an orator: 'vociferating the virtues of his vegetable medicines, extolling the efficacy of his pills'. At about the same time White visited Dudley market and interviewed another 'doctor' who declared he had been curing people with his herbal pills for twenty-five years: 'and you'll find 'em expel, eradicate and destroy, all the sluggish phlegm and slime which undermine and injure the principles of health'.

Nursing developed in the mid-nineteenth century and the best-known nurse in the region was Sister Dora, the 'Black Country Florence Nightingale'. Christened Dorothy Pattison, Dora was to leave an indelible mark on nursing care in Walsall. In 1864 Dorothy joined the Sisterhood of the Good Samaritan and took the name Sister Dora. She began work at Walsall's new cottage hospital in Bridge Street and was involved in caring for the victims of a number of industrial accidents. In 1872 at nearby Pelsall Colliery, for example, twenty-two men were trapped underground and Sister Dora rushed to the scene to render whatever help she could, providing food and blankets. She worked in Walsall for fourteen years before sadly dying of breast cancer. Today, Dora and her achievements are commemorated in the town with a statue.

Much has been written about Sister Dora over the years. A search of Walsall Library Service has revealed books and documents dating from 1880, including biographies by Margaret Lonsdale (1880) and Jo Manton (1971). Walsall Local History Centre has an archive of relevant documents (Ref No: 1154/2/13) and also material that can be accessed online at: www2.walsall.gov.uk/localhistorycentre/Local_Heritage/worthies/sister-dora.asp.

Statue of Sister Dora, Walsall town centre. (Author's photograph)

Hospitals

In almost all workhouses there was an infirmary to care for sick inmates. Each Poor Law Union had to employ at least one qualified medical officer to care for the poor, both those inside the workhouse and those receiving outside relief. Until 1863 nursing care in the workhouse was provided by female inmates, who were often unable to read the labels on medicine bottles. In the 1860s there was pressure to improve medical care. In Liverpool, as part of an experiment, a number of trained nurses and able-bodied female inmates began nursing together in a workhouse infirmary, with training provided on an in-house basis. This system was deemed a success and eventually spread to all union infirmaries in the country.

Whenever someone was admitted into a workhouse they were initially placed in a receiving ward, where they were examined to check their state of health. Anyone suffering an infectious disease was placed in a sick ward. Part of the initial process was to strip, bathe and issue uniform to the inmate. Their own clothes were washed and stored, to be handed

The former workhouse at Wordsley. (Author's photograph)

back on release. Families admitted together could only be released together, and were often split up into different wards in the workhouse.

Edwin Chadwick was a social reformer who became Secretary to the Poor Law Commissioners. In 1839 he conducted a survey on the state of health of the labouring classes. He concluded that lack of drainage, poor water supply and overcrowding were causes of the high death rate and short life expectancy.

Health provision in Wolverhampton, for example, had not grown commensurately with the population and needed to be overhauled. When Wolverhampton Dispensary opened in 1821, it dealt with a population of 18,000, but by 1840 the numbers had increased to almost 48,000. In 1843 a donation of £100 was offered by GB Thorneycroft, of Shrubbery Iron Works, to help establish a general hospital in the town. In 1844 a fund was started for the proposed hospital, and South Staffordshire General Hospital opened on 1 January 1849. It provided eighty beds and was built for a total cost of £18,898. The building was of stone and brick in the Italianate and Roman Doric style. The hospital cleaned its linen, baked its bread and also brewed beer – resident staff (doctors, nurses and servants) received a daily allowance of two pints of beer.

Provision was not free and patients were admitted on subscribers' tickets and without one of these a person could not be treated. A ticket was obtained by a subscription of 5s 6d, and the subscriber could use it himself or give it to a deserving person. Many influential people subscribed and gave tickets to employees or, in the case of church officials, to members of the congregation. Servants of existing subscribers were admitted on their master's payment of 1s 6d per day. There were charitable admissions for those who could not afford to pay, with approval of the Board of Management.

At times the hospital suffered through fluctuations in income. In 1854, for example, the number of beds had to be reduced to thirty and two wards were closed. In 1861 a sick children's department opened, followed by an isolation block in 1872. Accommodation was made available for medical pupils in the same year. In 1873 the Royal College of Surgeons 'recognised' the hospital as a medical training school. In 1928 King George V decreed that the hospital should henceforth be known as the Royal Hospital. More information on the development of the hospital is available at: www.localhistory.scit.wlv.ac.uk/articles/RoyalHospital/RoyalHospital.htm.

In nearby Dudley, 25 October 1871 was a fete day to celebrate the opening of the Guest Hospital, Tipton Road. There were flags and a procession, and the whole town turned out to honour the Earl and

Dudley Guest Hospital. (Author's photograph)

Countess of Dudley and the late Joseph Guest, a local chain maker who the hospital was named after. The Earl presented £30,000, in addition to many thousands he had already donated. Joseph Guest had died in 1867 and had donated £20,000 for the hospital, one of a number of gifts he made to local medical and educational causes.

The Guest Hospital occupied buildings erected some years previously for a blind asylum, established specifically to provide for those who had lost their sight in the pits. It had been built by the Earl of Dudley, who owned many pits in and around the town. The building had stood unoccupied for years as most potential inhabitants preferred to take a small pension and live in their own homes with their family.

The hospital contained fifty beds and a children's ward and was well laid out with views of Dudley Castle. The Earl spoke at the opening ceremony and reminded the audience that the hospital would only succeed with subscriptions and donations from the public. Noah Hingley, the Mayor of Dudley, also gave a speech in which he thanked the Earl for his generosity towards the hospital and other facilities in the town. The Guest still stands and is in use today as an out-patients' centre.

The hospital records database can be accessed at: www.national archives.gov.uk/hospitalrecords, and searches can be done online with the name of the hospital or in a particular place, and the results give details of where archive records can be found. A general search term such as 'lunatic' will reveal many results, so it pays to experiment with the specific name used for the establishment.

The Workhouse and Poor Laws

Workhouses were still remembered in relatively recent times through the buildings they occupied and the effect they had on inmates. Many workhouses were converted into hospitals, for example, Burton Road Hospital in Dudley and Wordsley Hospital in Stourbridge both started life as workhouses. There are examples in my family of elderly relatives who did not want to be admitted to the workhouse at Burton Road, and pleaded to be taken elsewhere, such was the stigma of the workhouse. Such attitudes persisted long after the demise of these institutions.

The earliest legislation dealing with the poor was the Statute of Cambridge in 1388, which stipulated that each 'hundred' (geographic district) must look after its 'impotent poor'. These people had to remain in their hundred and wear a badge showing which parish they belonged to. There were Poor Law Acts in 1597 and 1601 and an Act of Settlement in 1662, which gave the responsibility for the poor to the parish. The unpaid overseers had to collect rates from occupiers of land and property. They were to spend that money helping the destitute, apprenticing their children and getting the able-bodied poor back to work. From about 1700 joint union workhouses started to replace 'outdoor' relief.

By 1782 workhouses had become expensive to run and Poor Law reformer Thomas Gilbert presented what became Gilbert's Act in that year: 'for the Better Relief and Employment of the Poor'. The Act allowed outdoor relief for the able-bodied and workhouse places for the old and infirm. By 1795 there was need for further reform, which led to the 'Speenhamland System', not legislation, but a method of giving relief to the poor based on the price of bread and the number of children a man had. A series of bad harvests, population growth and the French Wars had led to a rise in the price of bread and famine was a real danger. Following a number of food riots in England in 1795, the system, it is said, helped to avert revolution in England, as had happened in France.

The first workhouse in Wolverhampton, located in Workhouse Lane until 1839, was visited by Sir Frederick Morton Eden in 1797. He described the inmates: 'Of 131 persons, about 60 are children … And others, either infirm, old or insane' (*The State of the Poor, or a History of the Labouring Classes in England*) (3 vols, 1797).

In 1832 a Royal Commission on the Poor Laws devised a way to eradicate pauperism at minimal cost. It proposed to make workhouse conditions worse than those of the lowest class of labourer outside. Outdoor relief was to be phased out, and those receiving indoor relief were to be made to feel like unwelcome guests. One of the common tasks allotted to the inmates of Wolverhampton workhouse, and elsewhere, was the breaking of stone. Anyone who refused to carry out this degrading task was fed on bread and water until they complied.

The *British Medical Journal* (www.bmj.com) is a useful source when researching the conditions in the workhouse, as well as all other medical queries. Articles from previous issues can be read online in PDF format and go back to 1840; access is free. There is also an excellent search facility on the website.

Researching pauper ancestors is easier because of the 1834 Poor Law Amendment Act, when Poor Law Unions were established. As a result, previous arrangements were combined, a local Board of Guardians was appointed and record keeping became more consistent. The best places to research workhouse ancestors are the local archives. Dudley has a wealth of documents, including minute books, ledgers, admission and discharge records. Stourbridge Library holds records covering Halesowen and Stourbridge workhouses. West Bromwich, Walsall and Wolverhampton all contain similar material.

There is a helpful guide to researching the poor and the Poor Laws on the TNA website at: www.nationalarchives.gov.uk/records/research-guides/poor-laws.htm. An online resource that is particularly useful when researching the conditions workhouse ancestors may have lived in is at: www.workhouses.org.uk. The site is managed by Peter Higginbotham, author of several books on the subject, including *Life in a Victorian Workhouse* (2011).

In addition, Jeremy Gibson and Colin Rogers's *Poor Law Union Records: 2. The Midlands and Northern England* (2008) covers Staffordshire and Worcestershire, and lists what resources are available at each archive as well as a great deal of information and advice. The table below gives an overview of Poor Law Union records and their availability, although it is not a complete list of what is held at each archive. Please note that some of the records are incomplete. Also, it is advisable to check before visiting any of the archives to ensure that records are available for the period you are interested in.

Poor Law Union Records at Black Country Archives

Dudley Covers Dudley, Sedgley, Tipton and Rowley Regis parishes	Poor Law Union minute books Ledgers Letter books Registers of admission and discharge Register of religious creed Registers of pauper lunatics
Stourbridge Some records at Worcester Covers Halesowen, Cradley, Old Swinford and Stourbridge – part Staffordshire, part Worcestershire	Overseers of the Poor records Registers of admission and discharge Poor Law Union minute books Workhouse Master's reports Pauper classification books
Stafford Worth checking which specific records are at Stafford Covers the area of the Black Country north and west of Dudley	Registers of admission and discharge Relief lists Removal orders Poor Rate books
Walsall Many records have been destroyed or are not yet traced Late-dated books can be found at Walsall Council Public Assistance Department and may be subject to Data Protection	Register of lunatics Poor Law Union minute books Some late-dated minute books (no admission or discharge details)
Walsall and West Bromwich Combined workhouse school between the two unions	Records for Wigmore School
West Bromwich Registers have not survived for the West Bromwich workhouse	Poor Law Union minute books Assessment committee minutes
Wolverhampton Covers Wolverhampton, Bilston, Wednesfield and Willenhall	Guardian minute books Multiple committee minute books Extracts from Bilston Workhouse register Workhouse Masters report and journal

Asylums

In the seventeenth century asylums were funded by charity and many were located in private houses. Inmates were paid for either by the parish or their relatives. In 1808 the Lunatics Act allowed county magistrates to fund new asylums from the rates. The Lunacy Acts of 1845 and 1890 impacted on how people were dealt with by authorities as it now became mandatory to build county asylums and set up a Board of Commissioners in Lunacy. There was also a proper licensing system for private institutions. The 1845 Act also created the central Lunacy Inspectorate and stipulated that 'lunatics' were to be treated as patients and housed in asylums, which had to register with the Commissioners in Lunacy. The asylum was meant to be an alternative to gaol or the workhouse and each asylum had to have a resident physician. The legislation also set out procedures covering admission, diagnosis and justification for admitting and keeping patients.

By 1847 there were 21 public asylums, and by 1914 this number had risen to 102. Many asylums were in use until the 1960s, when most became obsolete as a result of better medication and treatment. Some conditions, such as epilepsy and learning difficulties, were initially treated in asylums, but this changed as both asylums and medical understanding developed. Conditions in asylums were often better than patients would have had at home – there were modern facilities, good food and spacious surroundings. However, patients were in large wards, with up to fifty patients in each, and privacy and personal space were limited. Visiting was strictly regulated. Treatments did develop in the twentieth century, but included injecting chemicals such as morphine, bromide and digitalis; electric shock; and hot/cold shower baths.

The person responsible for the asylum was the superintendent, who was always medically qualified. He was assisted by a matron, who in the early days may have been his wife. A local visiting committee, drawn from magistrates, gentry, local nobility and the like, would oversee the asylum. Superintendents' reports are a good source of information and many of these can be found in local archives.

Specialist asylums were also established, such as 'idiot children's asylums'. A local example was the Midlands Idiot Asylum at Knowle in Warwickshire, which was built in 1872. These types of asylums were designed as long-term homes for children with learning difficulties and were conducive to learning and play. Other specialist asylums included epilepsy colonies.

Sandwell Hall was once the seat of the wealthy Dartmouth family but by the end of the nineteenth century it was being used as an asylum, the Sandwell Hall Industrial School for Mentally Defective Boys. This was a place for outcasts from society and the children probably had a wide range of behavioural and social problems. A large staff was employed to take care of 'inmates'.

Dudley Archives hold a register of pauper lunatics in various asylums, chargeable to Dudley Union; dates range from 1859 to 1913. The volume has a name index, admission dates and details of which asylums individuals were sent to. The main asylums are Stafford County (Stafford), Worcester (Powick) and Bromsgrove (Barnsley Hall). In addition, some individuals were sent out of the region, as far away as Lancaster. There is a useful index of asylums and mental hospitals at: www.studymore. org.uk/4_13_ta.htm. The Wellcome Library houses many documents and rare books on medical subjects, including superintendents' reports (for example, for Worcester Asylum) and is open to the public. There is a useful search facility on the library's website at: http://library.wellcome. ac.uk/index.html.

The Glenside Museum in Bristol is dedicated to psychiatric and learning disability hospitals; for further information access its website at: www. glensidemuseum.org.uk. A visit will give greater understanding of what it was like to be a patient in an asylum. A useful publication on the subject is Sarah Rutherford's *The Victorian Asylum* (2008).

Education and Institutions

Early education provision was very patchy and not controlled or assessed by the government. In the 1840s children as young as 7 were working underground in mines, as well as in other jobs. Children's Employment and Midlands Mining Commission reports acknowledged and were surprised at the lack of education, for example, many boys had not heard of London or even Queen Victoria. Any education was usually provided through charity schools, which relied on bequests and grants. Many grammar schools were established in this way, such as Dudley Grammar School (1562–1975). Dudley admitted boys free of charge, but by the nineteenth century many grammar schools were forced to start charging for pupils to attend, either as boarders or day pupils. As a result, some of these schools became residential public schools, such as those in Stourbridge: Old Swinford Hospital School and King Edward VI Sixth Form College, one of the oldest active schools in England. Wolverhampton

Old Swinford Hospital School, Stourbridge. (Author's photograph)

Grammar School was founded in 1515 having been endowed by Sir Stephen Jenyns in a trust deed of that year. The original school was in St John's Street, until it moved to Compton Road in 1875.

Dudley Grammar School survived the English Civil War, the Industrial Revolution, the beginnings and rise of local government and increasing government intervention in education. It finally ceased to exist in September 1975, when it merged with the three other Dudley schools to form the Dudley School as part of the birth of the comprehensive education system. The *Express and Star* newspaper reported events on the last day, 24 July 1975: 'Traffic came to a stop yesterday in Castle Street as more than 400 Dudley Grammar School boys made their way to St Edmund's Church for the school's final commemoration service. It ceased to exist yesterday – the last day of term after 413 years history.' Dr Trevor Raybould's *Dudley Grammar School 1562–1975* (2010) provides a full history of the school.

Education for those who could not afford it was provided in part by the ragged schools system, so called because many of the children who attended wore ragged clothes and had no shoes. These schools originated in London in the late eighteenth century, and outside London one of the first was set up by John Pounds in Portsmouth. Lord Shaftesbury formed the Ragged School Union in 1844, and at its peak there were 192 schools in England. Over time the schools declined and some were absorbed into the national education system. There were ragged schools in Two Gates in Cradley, at Stonefield in Bilston, Chance's (glassmakers) in Smethwick, at Netherend Chapel in Cradley, in Wolverhampton and Walsall. There is a dedicated museum in London, housed in the capital's biggest ragged school, which is open to the public. Further information is available on the museum's website at: www.raggedschoolmuseum.org.uk/nextgen.

In the early nineteenth century, Sunday school was one of the main forms of education available. In West Bromwich there was a gradual development of day and boarding schools. In the 1818 Staffordshire directory details of Lord Dartmouth's School at Black Lake are included, along with those of Edward Oxenbould, listed as a schoolmaster in High Street. Mrs Warwick ran an establishment for fifty boarding girls and there was a boy's boarding school at Sot's Hole. In addition, there were two national schools in the town.

Education began to develop further during Victorian times. In the 1840s in West Bromwich, Holy Trinity, the newly formed parish church, provided the first government-inspected school. The first inspection took place in 1844; there were 153 children on the role, with 98 regular attenders. Literacy was found to be poor and none of the children could

Cradley Ragged School. (Author's photograph)

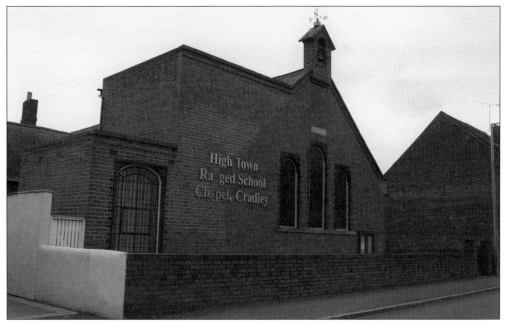

read 'with ease', although 46 (of 113 inspected) could 'make some sense of the words before them'. Few of the children could write. These details are taken from FW Hackwood's *History of West Bromwich* (1895, repr. 2010). More schools opened in the area, including another in West Bromwich, at Spon Lane by Kenrick's (Holloware Manufacturers) for the children of its employees.

The greatest change to education came in 1870 with the Forster Education Act, which stipulated that the needs of education as a whole should be considered. Local school boards were set up to ascertain how many children there were and to provide for their education. This led to expansion in schools, and pressure on parents to ensure their children attended. In West Bromwich over an 18-month period (1872–4) 500 parents were prosecuted for not sending their children to school.

School records may be found in the archives covering the local-authority area in which a school was located. Material may include admission and punishment registers, photographs, papers from various school logbooks, which are a diary of school events, including reasons for absence. There may be school board minutes, finance records and papers. Some of these records after 1910 may be closed because for Data Protection reasons. The National Trust Museum of Childhood at Sudbury in Derbyshire is a good source of information on education. It has eight galleries, each focusing on a different aspect of childhood, including work, home and school. It was transformed in 2008 following a £2.2 million redevelopment project. Details of the museum may be found on the Trust website at: www.nationaltrust.org.uk.

Other Education Providers
The Workers' Educational Association has been providing education for adults throughout the country for over a hundred years. It had a number of active branches in the Black Country, and these have now been amalgamated to form the West Midlands branch; for further information see the website at: www.westmidlands.wea.org.uk. The Co-operative Movement also played an important part in education from the mid-nineteenth century. The Co-op was not just about retailing, it also organised educational and social activities, including local sports days, seaside trips, drama groups and choirs (see chapter 6).

Food and Drink

Black Country food developed, in part, through the need to be thrifty. In rural areas food may have been more readily available as people could grow their own or may have acquired it from an employer. In the Black Country the market was the place to buy or the 'tommy shop', which resulted in poor quality and high prices. Rapid population increase and poor living conditions meant back gardens were yards and these were often not suitable for growing food.

The pig was very popular with Black Country people. It could be kept in a yard and was a staple part of the diet – it was said that every part of the pig could be cooked and eaten except the 'oink'! Pigs heads could often be bought cheaply or were even free. The brains were taken out and cooked and the head was boiled until the meat dropped off the bones, and this was then pressed to make 'brawn'. Other meat 'delicacies' were chitterlings (pig's small intestines), tripe (a cow's stomach lining) and heart (lamb, pig or cow). Rook breasts were used to make pies and wood pigeons (or even useless homing pigeons) were roasted or cooked in pies. No doubt many of these recipes were also popular outside the Black Country.

One particular Black Country dish was 'gray pays', filling food for the hard-working Black Country man or woman. It consisted of maple peas soaked overnight then simmered with bacon and served with bread. Groats, from oat cereal, kiln-dried to help remove the outer husks, were used with stewing beef to make 'grorty dick' or 'grorty pudding'. Groats could be ground to make oatmeal or used whole in stews. The recipe for 'boney pie' used bones from the butcher, boiled for 3 hours until the meat was tender and fell off the bone. This was then combined with onions and other vegetables and topped with pastry and baked. The leftover stock was used as a base for soup.

Some food items that have strong links with the Black Country include hot pork sandwiches; Black Country scratchings (pork rinds or, more uncommonly today, sold in a block); faggots and peas; bread pudding – 'fill belly'; pig's ear stuffed with a mixture of breadcrumbs, suet, beaten egg and herbs; jugged pigeon; and black (or pig's) pudding. Some of these are found elsewhere, for example, Bury in Lancashire is just as proud of its black pudding as the Black Country. 'Faggots and peas' have been made locally for generations and are still considered a Black Country speciality. Dried peas are soaked overnight before being steamed or slowly boiled. Neath in South Wales considers itself the 'faggot and peas capital of Wales', and the dish is also popular in Yorkshire and Lincolnshire.

Frumity (or frumenty) was wheat porridge made from the gleanings of the scattered ears of corn from corn harvest. These were made into miniature sheaves of corn and hung on the rafters until Mothering Sunday.

Then the grains were soaked in water for several hours, placed in a stew pot and cooked until quite soft, after which milk, sugar or treacle were added. It was eaten during the Sunday dinner. The recipe for frumenty dates from medieval times and sometimes other ingredients were added, such as meat or chicken, and it was also eaten at breakfast. Another traditional Mothering Sunday dish was roast veal and custard, or veal and milk gravy. The meal may have been finished off with a Simnel cake (Mothering cake), half boiled and then baked.

There are several publications that offer more information about Black Country recipes and food, including Pat Purcell's *Bostin' Fittle* (1978), available from the Black Country Society, and Marjorie Cashmore's *A Feast of Memories* (1986).

Resources

The *Black Country 1969* DVD (2010), produced by the Media Archive for Central England, contains programmes and ATV Today shorts from the late 1960s to the mid-1970s. A wide range of subjects is covered, including an interview with 90-year-old Hannah Baker, who lived in a condemned nineteenth-century end-terrace in Tipton with original grate and no electricity. Also featured are pieces on chain making and dog and cock fighting, as well as poetry, rhyme, songs and stills from around the region. It can be purchased from the MACE website at: www.macearchive. org. A total of three DVDs have been produced about Cradley in the *Cradley: Then and Now* series in addition to *A Story of Cradley Heath*; these are available from the following website: www.cradleyheathfilms.co.uk.

Chapter 6

THE BLACK COUNTRY OFF-DUTY

Introduction

It is easy to think that in the eighteenth and nineteenth centuries life in the Black Country was all about work and survival. However, there is plenty of evidence to show that life could be enjoyable and stimulating. Before television and radio there was live entertainment in theatres and music halls, and fetes and carnivals were enjoyed. Celebrations, such as the opening of Dudley Guest Hospital, often involved the whole town. The alehouse, beer house, inn and tavern were important social hubs, as were attractions such as Dudley Castle and Dudley Zoo, where thousands flocked in their downtime.

Holidays and travel of any kind were rare, but day trips by rail, bus or charabanc gave people a glimpse of the world outside the Black Country. Time spent hop picking in August was considered a holiday as it took place in the countryside in fresh air away from the dirt and noise of the Black Country. Sport was often brutal, reflecting the life being lived – bull baiting, dog fighting and prize fighting were all enjoyed and the breeding of fighting dogs was common. Racing pigeons was a popular pastime that continues today. Shopping, while not labelled 'retail therapy' as it sometimes is today, developed from the market and the 'tommy shop' and was strongly influence by the Co-operative Movement, which was prominent in the Black Country.

Local author Francis Brett Young gave glimpses of Black Country life through his books. Brett Young was the son of Dr Thomas Brett Young, the first Medical Officer for Halesowen, and he wrote a string of novels set in the Midlands between 1916 and 1938. He changed the names of towns, so that Halesowen became Halesbury, Dudley became Dulston and so on. The books are now out of print, but are regularly available on the Internet (via eBay, for example) and can be borrowed from local libraries. The Francis Brett Young Society website features a synopsis of each of his books and can be accessed at: www.fbysociety.co.uk. His

A postcard of Dudley market place, 1900s. (Author's collection)

first novel, *The Iron Age* (1916), was set in the Stour Valley in the Black Country, while *They Seek a Country* (1937) is the story of a nailer in Dulston.

Theatre, Cinema and Variety

The history of theatre and cinema in the Black Country is interesting, and mirrors what was going on across the country. Early theatre in Wolverhampton dates from the mid-eighteenth century, although not in a purpose-built theatre but at the town hall in Market Place. By the end of the century a theatre had been built behind the Swan Inn on High Green (now Queen Square on the site of Lloyds/TSB Bank). It remained open until September 1841, when a replacement was planned.

There were a large number of other theatres around the Black Country. The Theatre in the Old Square in Walsall, for example, was built by public subscription in the early 1800s; after a fire in 1845 it was converted into shops. In Smethwick the Theatre Royal opened in September 1897 followed a few years later by the Empire Variety Theatre in September 1910. On the opening night a series of pictures were shown, each set interspersed with variety turns. The building complied with the Cinemato-

Queen Square, Wolverhampton, 2012. Lloyds Bank can clearly be seen. (Author's photograph)

graph Act of 1909, which provided for public safety. The theatre could seat 1,500 and admission prices ranged from 2*d* to 1*s*. The theatre flourished and in 1919 was extended, with alterations to the stage and dressing rooms, ornamental plasterwork and re-decoration. The grand re-opening took place in October 1919 and artistes included Monsieur A Rossi's Musical Elephants, which played various instruments, including piano and trombone. Also on the bill was a ventriloquist, jugglers, a minstrel singer and Garner and Lee, who were described as 'eccentric comedians'. Variety at the Empire lasted until the 1920s, and it became exclusively a cinema from 1924 until its closure in 1957. In Dudley the most famous venue was Dudley Hippodrome, built on Castle Hill on the site of a former theatre, the Opera House, which opened in 1899 and burnt down in October 1936. Finally, in Stourbridge, the earliest theatre dated from about 1776. In 1793 the New Theatre opened and remained in business until 1850.

There were possibly as many as seventy or eighty theatres in the region from the eighteenth century. In addition, travelling theatres visited the area, such as the one owned by Bennett and Patch which operated from the 1840s. The Grapes, in Upper High Street, Wednesbury, a partially

111

re-built inn formerly known as the Green Man Tavern, is mentioned in Frederick William Hackwood's *Olden Wednesbury: Its Whims and Ways* (1899) as a place frequented by travelling players: '... was the rendezvous of every company of strolling players a century ago [in about 1800]. Remnants of the Thespian Temple used by these barn-stormers may still be pointed out at the rear of the premises.'

Today, the only significant theatre remaining in the Black Country is The Grand in Wolverhampton, which opened in December 1894. Over the years it has hosted many high-profile events and performers, such as Marlene Dietrich in 1962, an occasion that was talked about for decades afterwards. The venue fell on hard times in the 1960s and became a municipal theatre in 1969, while a Grand Theatre Trust was established in 1970. A decade later there were further financial problems, but The Grand was rescued and restored to its former glory. In 2011 it still draws crowds, not only from the Black Country, but also from Shropshire and Staffordshire. There are many records at Wolverhampton Archives and Local Studies Service relating to *The Grand*, including examples of posters and programmes, as well as an unpublished dissertation by Susan Fletcher, 'A History of the Grand Theatre, Wolverhampton' (document ref. DX872/2 in the archive).

Ned Williams's recently published book *Black Country Theatres* (2011) is the definitive work on Black Country theatres. Ned also published, simultaneously, a sister work, *Black Country Cinemas* (2011), which is very interesting and useful.

The development of cinema in the Black Country began in about 1898, two years after the Lumière Brothers' 'Cinematographe' was exhibited in London. The earliest recorded 'bioscope show', a travelling cinema, to visit the region was brought to Bilston by Captain Payne. It was only newsworthy because of a fire, which destroyed both Payne's equipment and the wagon used to transport it. The cinema age came about with the Cinematograph Act of 1909, which regulated cinemas and introduced licensing of premises showing films. The number of cinemas grew quickly, some in converted buildings, others in purpose-built venues, but mostly on a modest scale. In October 1928, in Brierley Hill, Oscar Deutsch built the first, brand-new, purpose-built cinema in the area, the Picture House; in 1936 it became an Odeon. In 1931 Deutsch opened his first Odeon, in Perry Barr, Birmingham; it is thought 'ODEON' stood for 'Oscar Deutsch Entertains Our Nation', though this has never been confirmed. Deutsch, born in Birmingham in 1893, created a chain of 258 Odeon cinemas, and their distinctive design was the work of Deutsch's wife, Lily, who created many of the splendid interiors. Oscar died at the young age of 48, in 1941. His wife sold the chain to J Arthur Rank and it was absorbed into the Rank Organisation.

Cinema attendance declined after the Second World War and many Black Country cinemas closed. A good number were converted into bingo halls, which ensured the preservation of the buildings. An example of this was Wood's Palace in Lichfield Street, Bilston. It had been an Odeon cinema, then closed and re-opened as a bingo hall and when this came to an end it was converted to a banqueting suite.

There has been a revival in cinema in recent years, with the growth and dominance of multi-screen cinemas. These offer choice to customers, possibly at the expense of individuality in terms of the architecture and surroundings – gone are the days of elegant cinemas, such as those built by Oscar Deutsch and his contemporaries.

For those interested in the history of theatres, the magazine *Old Theatres* is of great interest. A useful links page is included on the magazine's website at: www.oldtheatres.co.uk. The publishers of the magazine have also produced a book: Terry Kirtland's *Old Theatres of the Midlands*

The Limelight Cinema, Hartshill, now located at the Black Country Living Museum. (Author's photograph, courtesy of the BCLM)

(2008). Black Country archives contain many documents and photographs relating to theatres and cinemas in the region. The BCLM features the Limelight Cinema, a building that originally stood at Harts Hill, Brierley Hill from 1921. The cinema is in working condition and films shown include old favourites featuring the likes of Charlie Chaplin and Laurel and Hardy.

Wakes, Fetes and Celebrations

Originally a wake was a celebration held in honour of a saint to whom a church was dedicated. Such celebrations were usually held on Sunday (the only day of leisure), but over time the wake developed and grew. In Tipton following a candle-lit walk to the church and a service there was entertainment, and this gaiety and merriment lasted a whole week. Over the years the wake developed into an annual market. As more people moved to Tipton to work so the character of the wake changed. Bull baiting, dog fighting and other sports became part of the festivities and heavy drinking was commonplace – an 1869 bill poster described the wake as 'a "Great Bacchanalian Demonstration" held under the auspices of HRH King Alcohol'. This was not surprising as Tipton was in the heart of the mining and foundry area, where people worked long hours in difficult conditions. Life expectancy was as low as 23 years for the locals and as a consequence they played hard. Wakes developed into carnivals, which benefited local charities, and this change took place in part due to pressure from the authorities in the late nineteenth century. The wake/carnival in Tipton survived until 1959, when the Wakes Ground in Birch Street was acquired for a new ambulance station. Subsequently, it was felt that a great part of the town's heritage had been lost.

Fairs were also held and were similar to wakes in that they provided entertainment in the mid-nineteenth century. They were originally intended for the buying and selling of commodities, with an additional element of entertainment. Some of the earliest fairs were granted to Hales (Halesowen) and Walsall by Henry III in 1219.

Dudley Castle was an important recreational venue and at Whitsun each year a three-day fete was held here. In 1892 thousands of people attended and takings totalled £1,280, with the £700 profit split across good causes such as the Guest Hospital and Dudley School of Art. The band of the Coldstream Guards played, there was a hot-air balloon event, a Punch and Judy show, fireworks and much more. In 1916 trams from Birmingham and elsewhere organised special services to transport people to the event. As many as 20,000 people a day visited the fete. The castle keep was opened to visitors for 1*d* each and on a clear day seven counties as well as parts of Wales could be seen from here. The fetes died out after 1918, but the castle grounds remained open to the public. In 1937 Dudley Zoo opened in the grounds; at this time it was unique in that animals were not caged, but in enclosures. Within 18 months 1 million people had visited the zoo. The entrance turnstile is now listed as an early example of concrete architecture. For information on visiting the zoo and castle, and special events such as re-enactments at the castle, visit the website at: www.dudleyzoo.org.uk.

While the Black Country was often seen as a harsh place, efforts were made to introduce more cultural and stimulating activities. As a snapshot, in 1870 there were a range of such events around the region. The Corn Exchange in Stourbridge held a recital entitled 'A Night with Charles Dickens' by George Grossmith, a lecturer and comedy entertainer. Later that month the venue played host to Stanley Betjemen's London Opera, and various operas played to crowded audiences throughout the week. Howe and Cushing's Great American Circus and Menagerie also visited Stourbridge and set up in Foster Street, the current site of the bus

Entrance to Dudley Zoo. (Author's photograph)

station. It featured exotic exhibits, including camels, an elephant and a band of Amazons, performing wolves, bears and monkeys. Admission ranged from 2s to 6d.

There was organised entertainment across the Black Country, and this often took the form of spectacles. Amblecote held a Grand Annual Fete over two days every year, and in August 1905 Stanley Spencer's airship ascended each afternoon. Spencer used regular coal gas because it was much cheaper than hydrogen and was readily available. The airship was 80ft long and 35ft in diameter. Other entertainments were the band of the Scots Guards, the Stourbridge Prize Band, grand flower and cottagers' show and a firework display.

In the nineteenth century large families, low wages and uncertain employment were all factors that meant there was little opportunity to save for occasions such as Christmas. For those who fell on hard times

A painting, in oil, of Stourbridge High Street in 1897 by Edwin Grice. (Reproduced with kind permission of Dudley Museum and Art Gallery)

the workhouse was their only refuge. Christmas was a time for displaying a spirit of benevolence to the inmates of such establishments. The austere regime was relaxed and this was given publicity in local newspapers such as the *Stourbridge Observer*. In 1873 a report in the newspaper stated that it was agreed that the inmates of Stourbridge Workhouse would be regaled in the usual manner with roast beef and plum pudding on Christmas Day, and also given ale and tobacco. However, not everyone was treated equally at the workhouse at Christmas, as the workhouse master at Dudley reported: 'the inmates of the house thoroughly enjoyed themselves and an entertainment followed the dinner. The tramps were not regaled; they left at eleven o' clock having had a smell of the dinner'.

Pubs, Inns, Taverns and Breweries

A vast number of public houses existed in the Black Country – nailers, colliers and foundry workers were very thirsty customers, and the state of the water supply meant that beer was often the safest liquid to drink. In the 1830s in Coseley, for example, there were over fifty pits and those who worked there needed refreshment.

There are a number of public houses that you can visit today to get a flavour of Black Country life. The first is the Glynne Arms, better known as the 'Crooked House'. This is located on the very fringe of the Black Country, near the village of Himley. The Glynne family's manor was at Oak House Farm and they built the pub nearby. Sir Stephen Glynne was brother-in-law to William Ewart Gladstone. The building tilts some 15 degrees because of old mine workings beneath it, and this unusual feature has made it into a popular tourist attraction – a coin placed on the bar will appear to run uphill. The second public house worthy of mention is 'Ma Pardoe's' (the Old Swan) in Netherton. This is one of a few pubs where brewing still takes place on the premises, while the original painted tin ceiling in the bar is of interest too. It also serves traditional Black Country fare, including home-made faggots which are best served with mushy peas.

The brewing industry in the Black Country can be traced back to 1468, when the Borough of Halesowen licensed five 'common brewers'. Many churches were also brewers and the sale of 'church ale' raised money for church repairs, although this practice ended in about 1700. Beer and ale was also part of life in the workhouse and, as mentioned earlier, there was a brewery at the Royal Hospital in Wolverhampton. The beer brewed in the workhouse was very weak and probably safer to drink than the water because water used to make beer was boiled before brewing commenced.

In 1830 the Beerhouse Act was introduced as a measure to combat the evils of gin. Gin was cheap and potent and was drunk heavily by workers, some of whom had gin supplied as part of their wages. Beer was promoted as a more wholesome drink, and was obviously much weaker than gin. Home brewing in the Black Country was (and still is) a popular activity. From 1830 it was possible to make a living out of brewing beer, and there was a massive growth in small retail breweries. Some people not only brewed beer but also opened their houses as 'home-brew' houses. Over time, many smaller operators were taken over by larger breweries. Today three major companies dominate the market. Wolverhampton and Dudley Breweries grew by absorbing smaller concerns such as Julia Hanson and Sons, Netherton Old Brewery and thirteen others. Mitchell and Butler's have acquired almost forty smaller concerns since it was started by Henry Mitchell and William Butler. Ansell's grew out of a smaller number of breweries, including Thomas Plant and the Kates Hill Brewery.

Ma Pardoe's (the Old Swan), Netherton. (Author's photograph)

Despite the influence of the major concerns mentioned above, the local brewery industry is still thriving in the Black Country, with some of the best examples in the country, even the world, located here. Household names such as Ma Pardoe's, Batham's, Holdens and Sarah Hughes produce high-quality beer that is sold in pubs such as the Old Swan in Netherton (Ma Pardoe's), the Vine, aka the Bull and Bladder, at Brierley Hill (Batham's), the Park Inn, Woodsetton (Holdens) and the Beacon Hotel, Sedgley (Sarah Hughes).

A variety of resources are available to assist with research into Black Country breweries and public houses. Joseph McKenna's *Black Country Breweries* (2005) covers all the breweries that have existed in the region, together with the names of individual brewers and much more. A series of CD-ROMs on local pubs has been published by Tony Hitchmough; three CDs cover Sandwell, Dudley and Walsall/Wolverhampton and can be purchased at: www.longpull.co.uk. The Midland Pubs website at: www.midlandspubs.co.uk documents historic Midlands pubs, including many in the Black Country. While it is a developing website, it features many photographs, trade-directory information and has a

The Vine at Brierley Hill, aka the Bull and Bladder. (Author's photograph)

useful genealogy forum where queries can be posted. Other websites that are of interest can be found at: www.nationalbrewerycentre.co.uk and http://breweryhistory.com.

Temperance

The temperance movement that developed during the nineteenth century faced an uphill battle, as alcohol was a major release for hard-working men. Water and milk were often not fit to drink and beer was regarded as a safe beverage, but only if taken in moderate quantities. Initially, some temperance movements advocated not drinking spirits, but later total abstinence was promoted, as was a pledge not to offer alcohol to others. A women's temperance movement was formed with the aim of stopping men from drinking. In some areas as much as a quarter of family income was spent on alcohol.

Midland Temperance League Certificate of Merit, presented to Henry Pearson, the author's great-grandfather, in 1928. (Author's collection)

At Easter 1892 a 'great attraction' took place in Dudley to raise funds for the building of a temperance hall. Attractions included a collection of pictures, mechanical models and a bazaar in the public hall at the Mechanics Institute. The temperance movement was supported in its efforts by the churches and the Salvation Army. At this time miners were on strike in Netherton, and a Mr Hart addressed a crowd of 3,500 men and women at an open-air meeting. He suggested that the strikers would be more effective if they were teetotal and peaceable. This advice fell on deaf ears and the retort was, 'this is a miners' strike not a teetotaller's meeting'.

One manifestation of temperance in the Black Country was John Blackham's Pleasant Sunday Afternoon (PSA) movement. John believed that the way to divert men from the 'demon drink' was to offer them entertainment and education on their day off. He came from Hill Top in West Bromwich and was a leading light in the religious life of the town. He was a member of the Ebenezer Congregational Church and was made a deacon when he was only 29. Blackham began with a few friends by going around the streets of West Bromwich to persuade young men to join a meeting the following Sunday. A total of 120 young men turned up that day, and more came in subsequent weeks.

The PSA name came about as a result of a train journey made by John Blackham. In his carriage were a number of men who, by their conversation, made him think they were planning to have fun at his expense. To forestall what could have been a little embarrassing for him, John asked them the following question: 'What sort of Bible class would you rather have than go to a horse race or a cock fight?' They answered that they had nothing against the Bible, but did the services in church need to be so blessed dull? This answer caused John to use the word 'pleasant' when describing his meetings and so the name 'Pleasant Sunday Afternoon' was applied to the movement. So successful were these events that over the next ten years they spread throughout the Black Country. This success was followed by movements in the East Midlands and later in many other areas.

The PSA movement was not just about hymns and Bible readings. Over time it embraced flower shows, exhibitions, cycling, rambling, cricket and football clubs as well as popular Saturday night concerts. Mottos for the movement were 'Brief, Bright and Brotherly' and 'Sixty Minutes of Sunshine'. The room in Ebenezer Congregational Church, where the first meetings took place, was demolished in about 1906, but a plaque on a later building on the same spot records where Blackham started his life's work. It is believed that the PSA movement is still in operation in Australia, but there is little evidence of it in Britain nowadays.

Holidays and Excursions

In chapter 4 the growth and size of the tram network in the Black Country was discussed. Trams were also used to transport local people for leisure purposes. There was a tram from Amblecote to Kinver, for example, to take day trippers to the village in Staffordshire, which is still a popular tourist attraction today. The stop in Amblecote was outside the 'Fish Inn' (now a Chinese restaurant), and the route taken was unusual for trams because for about 1½ miles it ran across fields as it neared Kinver, it crossed the Stour at several wooden bridges and followed the Staffordshire and Worcestershire Canal at one point. It opened in 1901 and ceased in 1930, one of the last tram services to close in the Black Country. On Whit Monday in 1905 it carried 16,699 passengers, its highest number in a single day.

In the early twentieth century it was common for Black Country families to take a 'hoppen train' into Worcestershire and Herefordshire. They would stay at farms in places such as Callow End, Leighcourt, Knightwick and Stoke Edith in Worcestershire and Cradley near Hereford in order to pick hops. Children had a month-long holiday from school in August and 'gooenhoppen' ('going hop picking') was often their only break from the smoke and dust of the Black Country.

Hop pickers were housed in barns, barracks, cow sheds and even pigstys; cooking took place on log fires; and the earth toilets were very basic. The pickers had to rely on delivery vans for their food, and the nearest pub was often 3 or 4 miles away. However, these factors did not deter them and many regularly made the trek for their supper beer.

Strikes often took place among the hop pickers, mainly about how many bushels should be picked to the shilling, especially if the hops were small. The Midland workers regularly clashed with Gypsies, also employed by the farmers as pickers, and fierce battles took place between the two groups. By the 1960s times had changed, farmers had machines to gather the hops and more women went out to work. Families were also able to take holidays at seaside resorts, and it would not be long before package holidays lured people abroad to countries like Spain.

Bromyard and District Local History Society produced a useful history of hop picking a few years ago, *A Pocketful of Hops* (2007), and this has many references to the Black Country. Many of the hops grown in

Herefordshire were surplus to requirements locally, cider being the most popular drink in the area. In the early twentieth century, Perry Pudge of New House, Bishops Frome, sold pockets of hops, known as 'pudges', to small breweries in the Black Country.

As train services developed day tripping became popular. Regular destinations for Black Country residents were Stourport-on-Severn, Bewdley and Bridgnorth. One way to relive those experiences is by taking a journey on the Severn Valley Railway, from Kidderminster. Many people still regularly visit the places that were popular with their ancestors.

Traditional Black Country Sports

Prize fighting took place across Britain but was particularly popular in the Black Country. William Perry, better known as 'The Tipton Slasher', was probably the most famous of all fighters in the region and was

Statue of William Perry, Tipton Coronation Gardens. (Author's photograph)

a champion prize fighter between 1850 and 1857. He followed in his parents' footsteps working on narrow boats and quickly learned to fight. His early opponents were other boatmen, one of the spoils was by being the first boat through the locks. Perry established his reputation in 1836 by reportedly beating Birmingham pugilist Ben Spilsbury. Perry's nickname derived from his slashing round right-arm blow.

In 1857 Perry famously fought Tom Sayers, a man 5in shorter than him. Perry gambled his pub, furniture, rings and trophies on the fight but lost after only ten rounds. He died in 1880 and is buried in St John's Churchyard on Kates Hill, Dudley, latterly known as the church that was damaged during the Dudley earthquake in 2002. Further information about Perry can be found in Tom Langley's *The Tipton Slasher* (1971). A more recent account was written by Rob Davies and appears as a chapter in RH Davies's *Tales from the West Midlands Canals* (2010). A statue of Perry was unveiled in Tipton Coronation Gardens in Owen Street in May 1993.

Several Black Country nailers became notable prize fighters. William Small was the nephew of well-known fighter Jem Butler. Jem, nicknamed 'Darlaston's Glory', trained William. In 1836, when William was 24, he issued a challenge to anyone under 12 stone, living within 10 miles of Darlaston, to fight him to a finish, prize ring rules, for £20–25. Timer Hill was known as the 'Wolverhampton Pet' and he immediately accepted the challenge. Both men wanted to get into the London prize ring where big money could be made. Hill was supported by his employer, brass foundry owner John Nanney, who paid Hill's training expenses as well as his wages and that of his coach, Bill Baker.

The fight took place at Canwell Gate, 5 miles from Tamworth. This location was on the border of Staffordshire and Warwickshire and was chosen in case of police interference – they could quickly move over the county border to avoid any trouble. Small looked the stronger of the two – he was 5ft 9in, weighed 12 stone, had huge hands and was as 'durable as iron'; Hill was 5ft 7in, weighed 10½ stone, was less well built than Small, but looked the part. The ninth round of the fight effectively sealed the result in favour of Hill. He landed a blow on Small's nose, smashing it flat against his face, stunning him. This was quickly followed by a crashing right, with great force. Small fell to the ground and Hill dropped heavily across his stomach, knocking out all his breath. Small survived until round fifteen, when he was knocked out of the ring and rendered unconscious, unable to take any further part in this brutal fight. It had lasted just 23 minutes.

Small never fought anyone of note again. Hill went on to fight his trainer, Bill Baker, who defeated him in twenty-two rounds. This was to be Hill's last fight and within two years he died from pneumonia, aged 24. At his funeral William Perry was one of his pall bearers.

Another popular sport in the region, until about 1914, was bull baiting. There were bull rings at Sedgley, Halesowen, Darlaston and Wednesfield. At Lye,

> people used to climb on the tops of houses and walls to watch the baiting. If a bull could catch a dog on his horns, he would toss him high in the air ... If ever a dog pinned a bull's nose his owner would get a pound or two for him in no time. It made the bull roar terribly.

Bull baiting was declared illegal in 1825, but continued for many years afterwards. A bull stake was a feature in King Street, Darlaston until fairly recently; a plaque sited near to the stake's original location records its existence. Bear baiting took place at the Old Bell Inn, Bell Street during the Brierley Hill wake (first Sunday after 19 September), when the bull dogs that survived bull baiting were chosen to fight the bear.

Joe Mallen, born in Cradley Heath in 1891, had a major part to play in the story of the Staffordshire Bull Terrier. He was one of the founders of the first Staffordshire Bull Terrier Club in 1935. The club still exists today and its history is described on its website at: www.thesbtc.co.uk. The 'Staffie' weighs in at around 40lb, is much faster and more intelligent than the traditional Old English Bulldog and is also more tenacious, hence its suitability in the past for bull baiting and dog fighting. Joe died in 1975, but an interview with him is included on *The Black Country 1969* DVD (2010), produced by the Media Archive for Central England.

Cock fighting took place on a regular basis in Wednesbury as early as 1690. Horse fairs and wakes commonly had cock fights, which continued until at least the First World War, with irregular examples going on well into the twentieth century. The lectern in Wednesbury parish church has a fitting tribute to the sport, carved in the shape of a fighting cock and bearing the inscription,'The iron breasted, barrel chested, parson blest, cock-a-doodle-do'. A cockpit existed in Townwell Fold, Wolverhampton, one of the seediest alleys in the town, frequented by prostitutes and their clients and containing a number of brothels.

Some pubs in the late nineteenth century had 'rat pits', where dogs were put into cages 3–4ft in diameter containing as many as thirty rats. A good, tiny terrier was a very valuable dog. Some of the larger rat killings drew many spectators and had to move out into the street. This attracted the attention of the police and the principals were often arrested and the resulting court case usually ended in a large fine being imposed. There were still events being organised as late as the 1930s.

The best-known horse-racing venue in the Black Country is Dunstall Park, Wolverhampton. It opened in 1888 and prior to this from 1825 racing took place in the town at Broad Meadows. When the lease on the land expired the council bought it and turned it into a park. Dunstall Park was originally one of many racecourses in the Black Country, but now it is the only one still in existence. In the late 1980s there were plans to turn it into a retail park, but a £15 million investment secured its future and floodlighting was installed to allow evening races (the first such facility in England). A history of horse racing in Wolverhampton, covering both Broad Meadows and Dunstall Park, including photographs of the all-British Flying Event, which took place on the ground in June 1910, can be found at: www.localhistory.scit.wlv.ac.uk/Museum/OtherTrades/BCN/Racing.htm. There are many documents, including plans, relating to both racecourses in Wolverhampton at the Wolverhampton Archives and Local Studies Service. There is a photograph of the racecourse at Walsall at the Walsall Local History Centre.

Team Sports

During the late nineteenth century team sports began to develop and association football, rugby, cricket and athletics were very popular in the Black Country. Organised sports, such as cricket, were no longer the preserve of well-off young men and work teams as well as village and town cricket clubs were formed.

In 1876 association rules football separated from rugby football. Goldthorn Football Club was formed in 1876 and by 1880 it had become Wolverhampton Wanderers. In 1889 'Wolves' moved to the pleasure gardens at Molineux and the first official game played there was against the 'Villa'. The club, and their ground, have had their ups and downs during the twentieth century, but it is now flourishing once more. There are a number of histories of the club, including *Molineux Memories: 110 Years of the Wolves 1877–1987, and the 1988 Update*, by the 'North Banker' (1989). The North Bank at Molineux was one of the main stands but by the 1980s it was closed and derelict. Like much of the ground, it has been redeveloped to comply with regulations introduced following the Hillsborough disaster in 1989.

Other clubs that have made Football League status in the area are West Bromwich Albion and Walsall. Walsall's history dates from 1888 when

'Walsall Town Swifts' was formed from 'Walsall Town FC' (established 1877) and 'Walsall Swifts FC' (established 1879). West Bromwich Albion was formed in 1878 by workers from Salter's Spring Works in West Bromwich. They have played their home games at the Hawthorns from 1900. Albion was one of the founding members of the Football League in 1888. Histories of all the clubs mentioned here have been published over the years and can be sourced through bookshops and the Internet. Patrick Talbot's *White Shirt, Black Country* (2004) is a history of Black Country-born footballers who played for England.

There were many other clubs in the region, although they failed to reach the 'top flight' of league football. Most Black Country towns have had teams since the early days of association football, for example, Wednesbury Old Athletic, which existed from 1893 to 1924. Steve Carr has written a number of books about the club, the most recent of which is *The Old Uns Revisited* (2010); this is available as an eBook from Amazon.

In a similar way to football, cricket developed because of local and works teams. In 1892, at Trinity Schools, Old Hill, a concert took place in aid of the cricket club associated with Netherton Iron Works. A large audience listened to violin recitals and songs such as 'Darby and Joan'

Statue of Duncan Edwards, who was born in Dudley and was one of the 'Busby Babes' killed in the Munich air disaster in 1958. (Author's photograph)

127

and 'The Lost Chord'. Old Hill Cricket Club was formed in 1884 and is one of the most successful local clubs. It joined the Birmingham and District League in 1920 along with many other Black Country teams, including Halesowen, West Bromwich Dartmouth, Walsall and Wednesbury. A short history of the Old Hill Cricket Club is available on the club's website at: www.oldhillcc.co.uk.

Dudley cricket and football clubs shared a ground at the foot of Castle Hill. In 1985 both football and cricket teams were very successful in their respective leagues. On 25 May Dudley cricket team was preparing for a match against Aston Unity in a Birmingham League fixture when a large depression was found in the outfield. Later that day a 40ft hole had developed. Holes in Dudley are not uncommon, given the number of mine workings. In fact, on the sports ground shared by the two teams there had been twelve collapses since the 1930s. These holes were due to limestone mining, which entails the excavation of large caverns. This more recent occurrence was documented by Patrick Talbot and his account, along with photographs, can be found at viewed at: www.blackcountry society.co.uk/articles/holeinground.htm. Dudley Cricket Club folded after it lost its ground.

There is a great tradition of athletics in the Black Country. Tipton Harriers was established in 1910 and their most famous member was Jack Holden (1907–2004). Jack represented England in the international cross-country team from 1929 to 1939; broke the 30-mile world record in 1946; and was four times AAA marathon champion from 1947 to 1950. Jack also won the Commonwealth Games marathon in Auckland in 1950. Another well-known club is Wolverhampton and Bilston, formed more recently, and Dudley and Stourbridge Harriers, one of the oldest clubs in the area. It was founded in 1924 as Dudley Harriers, and amalgamated with Stourbridge, Wordsley and District Harriers in 1963. The club has been based at Dell Stadium, Bryce Road, Brierley Hill, since the cinder track was opened there in 1964.

Attractions

In the late nineteenth century, local authorities established public parks around the Black Country to enhance the lives of residents. Much land in the region was ravaged by mining and creating a park on some of that land was the start of regeneration. In May 1893, for example, 860 Tipton rate payers petitioned the Board of Health requesting the provision of a park. As a consequence, 35 acres of land was purchased between Randolls

Lane (now Victoria Road) and Park Lane East, at a price of £1,500, land that formerly had been used for mining. The construction of the park required the filling of mine shafts and the removal of a huge mound of spoil, which was used for building new road surfaces. Various gifts were received to enhance the park, including an iron drinking fountain and a children's gymnasium and shelter. The grand opening of the park took place on 29 July 1901, and was a day of great jubilation in Tipton. The festivities started with a procession accompanying the Earl of Dartmouth. This was followed by a luncheon in a large marquee erected on the cricket pitch and during this speeches and presentations were made. In 1921 the town war memorial was erected in the park in the form of an obelisk, and was unveiled by the Marquis of Cambridge. Today, the park is still a major part of Tipton life, and recently there has been further investment to improve the facilities available. The original drinking fountain still exists and the park is English Heritage grade II listed.

In September 1877 Broad Meadows, the former racecourse in Wolverhampton, was purchased by the council to build the first public park in the town. Originally known as 'The People's Park', it was later renamed

Ornate gates at the entrance to Stevens' Park, Stourbridge. (Author's photograph)

West Park when another facility was built to the east of the town. Over the years the park has been the venue for many events such as archery, cricket, bowls, flower shows and the Arts and Industrial Exhibition of 1902.

Many other parks exist in the Black Country, such as George Rose Park in Darlaston, which was created in 1924 and named after a local nut and bolt manufacturer. Mary Stevens Park in Stourbridge was named after one of its benefactors, Ernest and Mary Stevens. Ernest, a manufacturer of hollowware, was a well-known patron in and around Stourbridge, donating a number of parks as well as a maternity home. An account of his life and work can be found in Roy Peacock's *Ernest and Mary Stevens – The Continuing Legacy* (2007). This was published by the Thomas Pocklington Trust, and copies are still available from the Mary Stevens Centre in Oldswinford, Stourbridge.

Shopping

Shopping was very different in the eighteenth and nineteenth centuries. Miners were paid on Saturday after their shift finished, and often in the pub. This meant that their wives could not do their shopping until late in the day, sometimes as late as midnight. Saturday evening markets started in the early nineteenth century to cater for this. Later, payday changed to Friday, reducing the need for this type of market.

Markets are an old-established tradition in the Black Country. Hales-owen had a Sunday market going back 800 years by a cross in the Cornbow; the cross is now in the churchyard. During the 1960s re-development took place and a market hall opened in the new precinct, in the vicinity of the Cornbow. This closed a number of years ago and a supermarket has now been built there. Dudley and Stourbridge also held regular market days. The first Bilston market charter dates from 1328. In 1825 Parliament was petitioned to allow the village, one of the largest in Britain with a population of 14,000, to hold a weekly market in a public place and Royal Assent for this was accordingly granted. By 1891 demand for the market had grown and a spacious indoor market was created, and became a popular addition to the town. Initially, it opened until mid-night, like the shops in Bilston, but after the First World War hours were modified to 9pm on Saturday and 8pm on Monday. With no refrigeration meat and fish had to be sold quickly, and crowds would wait in the wings ready to jump in when the last joints of meat were being sold off. Nowadays, Bilston has a more modern market, but when it was first opened people complained it was not as good as the old facility.

In Wednesbury a market charter was issued by Queen Anne in 1709. It granted a weekly market on: 'Fridays in every week forever … for buying and selling corn, flesh, fish and other provisions, and cattle and beasts and all goods and wares and merchandise commonly bought in market places'.

The Co-operative Movement

The Rochdale Pioneers started the first cooperative in 1844, and the location of it is now the Rochdale Pioneers Museum. The Co-operative College website provides further details about the cooperative and the archive in Manchester, which has a wide range of records; it can be accessed at: www.co-op.ac.uk/about. A replica co-operative store can be found at Beamish Museum in County Durham (www.beamish.org.uk). Co-operative societies were interested in much more than simple retailing and undertook many other activities, including social events and educational projects. They organised local sports days, seaside trips, drama groups and choirs and provided reading rooms, libraries and meeting rooms. There was strong growth in many of the societies during their existence, although some found it difficult to become established, often because of financial problems. In Walsall, for example, a co-operative society was formed in 1862 but only lasted four years, although eventually a society was set up that remained in existence for a long time. Societies were formed through holding public meetings and by people pooling resources to establish enough capital to begin trading. A number of co-operative societies were created in the Black Country, for example, Halesowen and Hasbury (1870), Tipton (1871) and Dudley (1872). Through a series of amalgamations the various societies eventually became the Midlands Co-operative Society, which still exists today. Ned Williams's *The Co-op in Birmingham and the Black Country* (1993) examines the history of the Co-operative Movement in the Black Country (and Birmingham) comprehensively.

Newspapers

One of the earliest British newspapers was *The Times*, which was first published in 1785 as the *Daily Universal Register*. From 1712 to 1855 newsprint was heavily taxed but in 1835 this was reduced and finally removed in 1855, and as a result many new newspapers were established. The table below lists many of the newspapers that have covered the Black Country and are available at archives.

Newspapers Covering the Black Country

Newspaper	Published From/To
County Express	Various dates
Stourbridge News	1995 to present
Wolverhampton Chronicle and *Staffordshire Advertiser*	1789–1930
Brierley Hill Advertiser	1856-7
Dudley Herald (now *Dudley News*)	1866 to present
Cradley Heath and Stourbridge Observer	1864
Black Country Bugle	1973 to present
Dudley and District News	1880-5
Dudley Chronicle and County Advertiser	1910–35
Walsall Advertiser (and newspaper)	1862–1915
Walsall Free Press	1856–1903
Walsall Times and *South Staffs Observer*	1925–54
Express and Star (various editions)	1884 to present
Wolverhampton and Staffordshire Herald	1851–69
Weekly News for West Bromwich, Oldbury, Smethwick etc.	1879–1944
Bilston and Willenhall Times	1924–66
Bilston Herald	1871–82
Darlaston Weekly Times	1882-7

It is possible to search for newspaper locations on the Internet at: www. newsplan.co.uk. Click on the West Midlands part of the map, then go to the home page and click on the search link. Archives have some physical copies of newspapers, but many are on microfiche and microfilm. The British Newspaper Archive has many newspapers online at: www.british newspaperarchive.co.uk.

Chapter 7

RELIGION

Introduction

In this chapter religion in the Black Country is examined, specifically the development of the Anglican Church and the emergence of Non-conformity. In most areas of the Black Country the Anglican Church was first to develop, but in some places Nonconformity was first to emerge. Some of the earliest relevant records are those maintained by the parish, and details of where and how to use such records are given below.

John Wesley was a frequent visitor to the Black Country, and his visits were well recorded. He was not always welcomed and violence and riots often followed him around the country. However, he persevered, possibly as a consequence of his surviving a fire at his home in Epworth, Lincolnshire when he was just 6. Against the odds he escaped, a 'brand plucked from the burning', destined, according to his mother Susanna, for greater things.

Apart from parish registers, burial records can also be researched, and advice about trying to locate the graves of ancestors is given below. A great deal has been written about churches and religion in the Black Country and relevant sources are listed.

The Early Situation

One of the earliest names in Wolverhampton's history was Lady Wulfrun, or 'Wulfruna'. A Mercian noblewoman, Wulfruna was granted land in the area in 985 and is seen as the 'founding mother' of the town. In 994 she gave lands in Bilston, Willenhall and elsewhere to the monastery of Hamtun. The minster church was St Peter's, which celebrated its millennium in 1994. The original Anglo-Saxon church at St Peter's was replaced in the early thirteenth century and parts of it still form the base of the tower of the present building. Chris Upton's *A History of Wolverhampton* (1998) gives more information about Wulfruna and St Peter's.

The ruins of Dudley Priory. (Author's photograph)

A little-known hermitage was established in the forest of West Bromwich known as Sandwell (or Sanwell from 'sanctusfons' – holy well). Sandwell Priory was founded in about 1130 and dedicated to St Mary Magdalen. It was under the jurisdiction of the Bishop of Lichfield and there are occasional references to it in cathedral records. Nearby, in Dudley, Gervase Paganall was involved in the building of Dudley Priory (St James's) and land was set aside for it in the 1150s. The monks came from Wenlock Abbey and were given permission to quarry stone for the priory. Dudley Priory was confirmed in 1182 and remained a cell of Wenlock, with probably never more than six monks living there. More details of Dudley Priory can be found in John Hemingway's *An Illustrated Chronicle of the Castle and Barony of Dudley (1070–1753)*. No traces remain of Sandwell Priory, and Dudley lies in ruins.

The Established Church

From the Reformation until the early nineteenth century most people belonged to the Church of England. In 1559 the Act of Uniformity made the Protestant Church the Established Church of England and forced Dissenters, Roman Catholics and Jews to worship in secret. Ancestors who fell into these categories are unlikely to have been recorded in parish records, and perhaps the only official references to them may be in court records for disobedience. Ministers who regularly preached outside the sermons laid out in the Official Prayer Book could find themselves sentenced to life imprisonment. Parishioners who refused to attend their parish church for more than one month were also liable to imprisonment.

The English Civil War (1642–51) brought about much change, and Dissenters were once again free to meet. Evangelists went around the country attracting new converts and people moved between churches more readily, sometimes because of news of a new minister, who could cause a split because of his emphasis on different aspects of the faith of the Church. At the end of the war came the Restoration of Charles II and the downfall of the Puritans.

Until the 1870s there were periods when certain Nonconformists were either persecuted or tolerated, but in 1851 17 per cent of the population in England belonged to a Nonconformist church. As a result of persecution many Nonconformist churches kept few records, in particular the Roman Catholic church, although the Quakers are an exception to this. An ancestor's absence from the parish baptismal register may indicate that they were a Nonconformist.

Anglicanism

The Anglican clergy were important from the Middle Ages and their lives have been well recorded. Many families will have Anglican ministers in their family tree, and it is worth bearing in mind that Anglican families may have moved around the country. A feature of the Anglican ministry is that its clergy had to be educated, tested and ordained, and thorough records were kept of these processes. The Clergy of the Church of England Database website makes available and searchable the principal records of clerical careers from over fifty archives in England and Wales, and is accessed at: www.theclergydatabase.org.uk.

Once a vicar or rector arrived in a parish he would live close to his church. He had social standing, which meant he was often chosen to sit as a magistrate in the local petty sessions, as well as other roles where records were kept, such as the Board of Health and workhouse chaplain. It was not only the gentry who entered the Church, there are many examples of shopkeepers and labourers making a career in the Church.

135

Dudley is blessed with two parish churches, St Thomas's and St Edmund's. The medieval church of St Edmund's was demolished in 1646 and little is known about it. From 1720 planning began for its replacement. Building was started in 1724 when John Homer laid the first brick at the south-west end of the church – it was inscribed 'The first brick laid by John Homer'. The new church was finally completed in 1739. It meant a lot to the people of Dudley and many leading families in the town were associated with it, Dixon, Finch, Amphlett, Hawkes and Wainwright to name but a few. St Thomas's, known locally as 'Top Church', was also re-built, by order of the vicar Dr Luke Booker. The old, medieval church was demolished in 1815 and the new church completed in 1818.

Cradley parish church came about due to the misfortune of the Nonconformist Congregational Church, which was declared bankrupt in 1798. In May of that year a petition was presented to the Bishop of Worcester signed by the Lords Lyttleton, Dudley and Dartmouth, as well as many inhabitants of Cradley and neighbouring clergy. It sought to bring the Congregational building into the Established Church. The petition highlighted the fact that Cradley had become a sizeable township as a result of coal and iron mining and was remote from other parish churches at Old Swinford, Kingswinford, Dudley, Rowley and Halesowen. The petition was accepted, the Independent Society disbanded and alterations were begun on the chapel – the dimensions were enlarged, the vestry raised and converted into a chancel and 'elegant Pulpit furniture' installed (*James Scott Manuscript 1800–1826*, published by Scott in about 1827 as *A History of Cradley, 1800–1826*). The other Nonconformist churches in Cradley were Presbyterian, Methodist, and Baptist, which met at the house of Thomas Hilditch. There were also a number of lay ministries, such as Joseph Haden's Independent Church, formed in 1787.

In Cradley there is much evidence of co-operation between the different congregations in the early days. Later in the nineteenth century division and rivalry surfaced and this lasted into the twentieth century. The relationship between the Anglican Church and Nonconformists was strained, each being suspicious of the other. Some co-operation was achieved between the Nonconformists through the Cradley Free Church Council, formed in 1896. By 1926 relations with the Anglican Church had improved considerably but links with Catholic and Anglo-Catholic movements were poor. This is evidenced by a conference held in June of that year where rigorous action against the Catholic Church was called for.

St Thomas's Church, 'Top Church', Dudley. (Author's photograph)

Cradley St Peter's Church, which was Cradley Chapel. (Author's collection)

Margaret Bradley and Barry Blunt have written a series of useful books about Cradley churches, *The History of Cradley Churches Part one: 1700–1800* (1998); *Part two: 1800–1900* (1999); and *Part three 1900–2000* (2000). These publications are available from the very useful Cradleylinks website at: www.cradleylinks.co.uk.

The Emergence of Nonconformity

Nonconformists are those who prefer to remain outside the Church of England, although their general approach to Christian Belief is the same. There are important differences in the way they worship, for example, bowing at the name of Jesus and kneeling to receive Communion. As previously mentioned, the period of the English Civil War was pivotal in the history of Nonconformity and early Nonconformists from that period are usually called Puritans.

Following the English Civil War and the Restoration of Charles II in 1660, the new Parliament wanted to reinstate the power of the Anglican Church. Puritan ministers disagreed with the terms of the Anglican Church and about 2,000 Puritan ministers were ejected from their parishes. According to the Revd James Scott there were twelve such ministers preaching within 4 miles of Stourbridge.

For the next few years the Puritans went from being persecuted and being made permanent outsiders to being tolerated. In 1689 the Toleration Act allowed Dissenters to worship in their own meeting house, as long as they obtained a licence from the Bishop and swore an oath of loyalty to the Crown at the Quarter Sessions. In 1691 Nonconformists were officially allowed to establish chapels and by the end of that year most market towns had at least one Nonconformist church.

During the early eighteenth century, when George I ascended the throne, a series of riots occurred. The Tories and the Church believed that Dissenters were weakening the influence of the Church of England, putting it in grave danger. There was a large Whig (Liberal) majority in Parliament, which added to Tory and clergy fears. The riots around the country were aimed at Dissenting ministers. The Pensnett Meeting House was one target of rioters and was burnt down on 17 July 1715. A new building was constructed on the site in 1716, paid for by the government. This followed the passing of the Riot Act in 1715, which made destruction of meeting houses a felony.

During the 1700s Nonconformist numbers declined, but from the 1730s John Wesley and George Whitefield preached a new personal, vibrant form of Christianity. They established the Methodists, so-called because they persuaded people to live their religion according to a new 'method'. By the time of Wesley's death in 1791 the Methodists had broken away from the Church of England, even though there was no theological difference in Methodist and Anglican beliefs.

During the period of the Industrial Revolution the gulf between Non-conformists and Anglicans grew. Small tradesmen joined Nonconformist churches and resented Anglican control of public life. The tradesmen were seen by government as becoming more powerful and it began to take account of their religious opinions in areas such as Poor Law reform, registration of births, deaths and marriages and the institution of borough cemeteries. These were all worked for by the Nonconformists to weaken the Anglican position.

Lye Waste was described in the following way: 'rude settlement [separated] from the rest of the hamlet and parish, a more marked distinction in manners and in the general state of society could scarcely have subsisted' (William Scott, *Stourbridge and its Vicinity* (1832)). Attempts to introduce religion to Lye Waste by Calvinists and Methodists failed to the extent that preachers regularly met with violence from locals. In

1790, the Revd James Scott did manage to open a room for religious worship in Lye Waste and he and other Unitarians held a Sunday school and Sunday evening lectures there. These activities were often interrupted by violence and it wasn't until 1806 that the first chapel was opened on the Waste. Unusually, here the Established Church followed in the wake of the Nonconformists when Christ Church was built in 1813 between Lye and Lye Waste. It was consecrated in 1843 when the Revd Henry Hill became its first incumbent. This example and the earlier one at Cradley are in one way extraordinary. In many parts of the country the Evangelical Revival had weakened the Church of England, as Nonconformists had split from the Established Church. In Lye Waste and Cradley the Nonconformists were the first to become established.

Another major change to the religious landscape came about as a result of the Industrial Revolution. Population distribution around the country changed and areas such as the Black Country were transformed. Many new, or newly changed, towns and cities had no Anglican church. The Nonconformists attracted huge numbers of converts, and in the 1851 ecclesiastical census more than half of those who attended church in the Black Country actually did so at Nonconformist chapels. It is important to point out that about two-thirds of the population attended no religious services at all.

The major branches of Nonconformity in the nineteenth century were Baptists, Congregationalists, Methodists, Mormons, Presbyterians, Quakers and 'others'. Most Nonconformists were middle class, while classic Anglicanism was more the preserve of the upper classes. Working-class involvement in the church was largely restricted to baptism, marriage and burial.

Methodism and Baptism

John Wesley made many visits to the Black Country. These included a total of thirty-three trips to Wednesbury alone between 1743 and 1790, more than anywhere else he visited. He also preached at Tipton Green between 1745 and 1752 and established the first Methodist chapel in Staffordshire on the site. John Wesley placed each member in a class with a leader to ensure their spiritual needs were met, as well as taking an interest in all other parts of their daily lives. Physical violence was often used against Wesley and his followers.

During the 1740s life was difficult for the Wednesbury Methodists. In February 1744 there were six days of rioting during which armed mobs systematically destroyed the property of known Methodists. Shopkeepers were among the worst affected and many lost their stock during the riots. The local magistrates refused to support the Methodists in their attempts to obtain warrants against the rioters, but they also declined to take action against the rioters. At the age of 86 Wesley made his last visit to the town, 'to our old friends at Wednesbury where the work of God greatly revives'; he died in 1791 less than a year later. Dr John Fletcher, founder member of the Black Country Society, wrote that Wednesbury typified many newly developed industrialised urban towns in that it had produced a population little affected by the traditional organisation of the Church of England; its size had doubled during the seventeenth century.

Interestingly, while it appears that some Wednesbury men, mainly miners, joined the rioting mobs, it was clear that others were from nearby Darlaston and Bilston and a few from Walsall. There was also evidence that a 'mob' from Wednesbury drove away a Darlaston gang intent on attacking Methodists. The riots did not destroy the determination of Methodists and the society grew, with many Wednesbury Methodists going out to other Black Country towns to find converts.

The violent response to Methodism might have been due to the Primitive Methodist belief that no one could be admitted who attended 'vain and worldly amusements, wastes his time at public houses, buys or sells smuggled goods . . .'. Methodists were expected to keep the Sabbath holy, while to many Black Country workers Sunday was their day off and many frequently spent it drinking beer, often to the extent that they were not fit to attend work on Monday. Edward Chitham's *The Black Country* (repr. 2009) devotes a chapter to eighteenth-century religion and industry.

Sunday School

Robert Raikes (1736–1811) is credited with promoting Sunday schools. These pre-dated state education, which became compulsory with the Education Act 1870. Many children worked six days a week, up to 12 hours a day, with Sunday being their day of rest. In 1781 Raikes started his first Sunday school in Gloucester and used the Bible as a textbook to teach children to read and write. Within 4 years 250,000 children were being educated around the country in this way. Sunday schools in industrial areas were supplemented by ragged schools (see chapter 5). Another 'version' of Sunday schools were the Socialist Sunday schools, which were formed as part of Labour Churches in 1892 and by 1912 numbered over 200. The first Socialist Sunday school in the Black Country appears to have been set up in Wolverhampton in about 1893. There is no specific record of how the Sunday school was begun, but one report talks of forty children gathering at an open-air Labour Church meeting in the town. The children returned the following week and a Socialist, Tom Frost, began reading the story of Cinderella to them. This account comes from the *Labour Prophet,* the paper of the Labour Church Union, and was written by Joseph Whittaker from Wolverhampton. Other Labour Churches formed in West Bromwich, Dudley and Stourbridge. As state education developed there was no diminishment of Sunday schools, but generally the emphasis shifted from basic education towards more community based activities, such as celebrating significant anniversaries and joining choirs.

In the 1920s the Princes End Baptist Sunday school treat was a visit to a field, either in nearby Coseley or Hurst Hill, where the children enjoyed races with small prizes followed by a picnic. One particularly memorable occasion for Hilda Francis, who attended the Sunday school, was a canal-boat trip to Ashmore Park in Wednesfield. This started at Mitchard's coal wharf in Bloomfield Road. The horse-drawn boat had to go through Coseley tunnel to reach its destination and the excited children shrieked as they were plunged into the darkness. The boat passed the Bilston land-mark Stewarts and Lloyds factory, where oily effluent had made a rainbow of colours over the water. Once the group arrived at Ashmore Park they found the 'park' was just a field (today it is a housing estate), but the usual races took place and one of the teachers also set up a sweetshop and the customary picnic of buns, cakes and lemonade was laid out.

For many people Sunday was chapel day and nothing would change that. There would be a morning Sunday school, followed by the chapel service, then afternoon Sunday school and finally an evening family service. WL Pace went to Short Heath Methodist Sunday School from 1935 to 1944. It comprised about 130 children, split between the main school and a primary department. Pupils were awarded stars for each class attended. At the end of the year these were counted up and each child was awarded a prize, usually a book, categorised as first, second and third class, depending on levels of attendance. Many of these books are still in existence and the prize certificates they contain provide another glimpse of the lives led by previous generations.

There are many different records of individual Sunday schools available to read in the local archives around the Black Country. As schools were organised by a particular church it is helpful to know which church an ancestor attended to find the relevant records. The archives contain many photographs of anniversaries and choirs, as well as cashbooks and other written records.

Parish and Church Records

In the Black Country, especially during the period following the emergence of Nonconformity, biblical names were popular; in the nineteenth century names such as Titus, Noah, Isaiah and Job crop up regularly, probably as a result of the influence of evangelists such as John Wesley and others. The 1756 register of baptisms at St Mary's Church at Oldswinford records some unusual forenames, for example, Mehetabel (daughter of Joseph and Ann Morral), Caranappa (Holloway), 'Prince Henry Earp' and 'John Back Wenlock Ellis', as well as the more customary biblical names, such as Elisha, Samson and Cornelius.

Until 1837 tracking down Nonconformist records could be difficult. Where kept, ministers often retained their own records and took them with them when they moved around the country. One resource that may be of help is the *Register of Births of Children of Protestant Dissenters*. This was a voluntary register, set up in 1742, and from this date until 1837 there were almost 49,000 entries. These records are held at TNA (series RG 4 and RG 5), and can be viewed online at: www.thegenealogist.co.uk. Some people travelled a great distance to register their child, as this had to be done in person. Also contained in series RG 4 and RG 5 are records of the Wesleyan Methodists, a register that commenced in 1818 and closed in 1838. It is also worth checking with local family history societies for any independent records they might be aware of. The local society for the Black Country is the Birmingham & Midland Society for Genealogy & Heraldry (www.bmsgh.org), a large society with branches in Birmingham, Stourbridge and Wolverhampton.

Online the website www.freebmd.org.uk can help to find Non-conformists through searches of records held by TNA. Searching records is free, as is basic information, but full details require you to purchase credits and download a copy of the record to your computer. The data-base also contains records of Anglican clergyman. Alternatively, you could consult *Crockford's Clerical Directory*. This has been published since 1858 and while it doesn't give demographic information, such as dates of birth and death, it does provide career information. The individual's entry ceases on their death, so the first edition where they are not listed should normally indicate when they died.

Crockford's was pre-dated (from 1841) by the *Clergy List*, and while this is not as detailed as *Crockford's*, it is still useful. Prior to 1841 it is necessary to consult parish records for information, but it should be possible to find the date of arrival in the parish, as well as the date of leaving or death. Local bishop's registers usually give more detail on movements. *Crockford's* website only covers recent records and has a free search engine: www.crockford.org.uk. It also contains two links to sites that hold historical data. The first at: www.theclergydatabase.org.uk covers the period 1540–1835, while the second at: www.lambethpalace library.org is the historic library of the Archbishop of Canterbury and assists with searching later issues of *Crockford's*, as well as other printed sources, to answer queries.

The survival of early parish registers is very patchy; and often they contain scant information: baptisms may only yield the child's name, father's name and date of baptism, while wedding entries usually only have names of the spouses. After 1754 records of marriages were entered into a special register and contain more information. If an early ancestor had a common name, then care must be exercised to ensure the correct record is identified. The Familysearch database at: www.familysearch. org lists many births and marriages from parish registers under series RG 4-8.

If you cannot find the relevant parish register then it is worth inquiring about the corresponding Bishop's Transcript (BT), which should be a carbon copy of the parish register. However, a word of caution when using these, the quality of transcription was often poor because the people transcribing them were not paid for their work. The BTs were an annual return of baptisms, marriages and burials. Generally, they date from 1597, but there are some earlier records. The Diocese of Lichfield made returns every two years and this created large and bulky documents in industrial parishes, as was the case with many Black Country parish records.

Over the years boundaries have changed, but in 1541 there were twenty-two dioceses and there are now forty-three in England. A further complication is that a parish may be geographically in one diocese, but ecclesiastically in another. There are sometimes differences between BTs and parish records, and for many reasons the BTs are also an incomplete record. It is important, therefore, to consult both the parish records and the BTs when carrying out research. The northern part of the Black Country, including Walsall, Darlaston, West Bromwich and Wolverhampton, is in the Diocese of Lichfield. The southern part, for example, Halesowen, Dudley and Stourbridge, is in Worcester. To access the full list of parishes visit the Church of England website at: www.achurchnearyou.com and enter the postcode or town you want to search for. The lists are extensive and all Black Country parishes are recorded either in Worcestershire or Lichfield diocese.

Parish boundary maps can often be located at local archives, and a search of www.blackcountryhistory.org shows several maps, for example, St Matthew's, Walsall. One local website, www.sedgleymanor.com, has maps that show the location of local churches within their area. Genuki also has good resources on parishes countrywide, including Staffordshire and Worcestershire. A good place to start on the site is at: www.genuki. org.uk/big/eng/, and while there are no maps, there is plenty of information, including where parish records may be found. There is a description of each town in the county, taken from *The National Gazetteer of Great Britain and Ireland* (1868), as well as a church locator for each town, which displays results on a variety of online mapping systems. Most parish records and BTs are housed at the local archives. Cecil R Humphrey-Smith's *Phillimore Atlas and Index of Parish Registers* (3rd edn, 2002) is a useful publication. Locally, some of the parish records for Holy Trinity Church, Amblecote, are indexed online at: www.holytrinityamblecote. org.uk; the church's older records are at Dudley Archives.

A useful guide to parish registers, including Nonconformist records, is Simon Fowler's *Trace Your Ancestors* (2011). In addition, Ancestry has a map to assist in locating a parish and can be accessed at: www.ancestry. co.uk/parish. If you click on a county on this map, records and collections for it will be listed. Some records provide more than just information on significant dates for an ancestor, but can also reveal details of what life was like at the time, for example, deaths and significant events in the community may have been as a result of outbreaks of cholera or even plague, which will be recorded in parish records.

Civil Registration

Civil registration of births, marriages and deaths was introduced in 1837. Record offices hold the indexes of these records on microfiche, and these are the most important and, probably, the most accurate records available. Ordering a certificate is the only way to get access to full information and when doing so as much information as possible should be included. The indexes can searched and entries viewed in the register online at: www. freebmd.org.uk, but it is still necessary to order original certificates to gain all the information, and not all records have yet been indexed.

Similar indexes can be found on commercial sites, such as Ancestry and Findmypast.

Churches and Burial Grounds

Traditionally, burials took place in local parish churches. However, by the early nineteenth century many parish churchyards were full. Private companies began to operate some cemeteries and municipal authorities also opened cemeteries, usually on the outskirts of towns, where land was cheaper. Legislation was passed, the Burial Acts from 1852 to 1857, which established Burial Boards, introduced inspection of burial grounds and ensured that Burial Boards kept those burial grounds that had closed in good order. Burial Boards also provided new cemeteries as required. As burial often took place close to the place of death it is worth checking churches and public cemeteries near the place stated on the death certificate.

There may be useful records in the archives for Sickness and Burial Records Clubs, such as Wolverhampton & District Patients Aid Association, which can be found at Wolverhampton Archives and Local Studies Service. There is also a series of Black Country churchyard and cemetery websites, all linked and found at: www.blackcountrychurchyards.co.uk, and this includes a database and subscription facility to allow you to obtain photographs of gravestones. The sites cover Walsall, Sandwell and Dudley Metropolitan Borough areas.

The National Burial Index lists burial records and this information is published on CD-ROM by the Federation of Family History Societies and is available to purchase at: www.ffhs.org.uk; the latest version is dated 2010 and holds 18.4 million burial records. There are 800,000 Staffordshire and 542,000 Worcestershire records in the collection, but no monumental inscription data is included. Many burials can be found at Findmypast, and this is most accurate for dates after 1813.

If you have located a death certificate or burial register entry for an ancestor, more information can be uncovered by finding the grave or memorial. If there is a headstone, then the epitaph will be the last word on their life. You may also find information on other ancestors if there is a family grave. If you cannot find a gravestone, then it may be worth checking for a memorial plaque inside the church. Local authority websites are a useful starting point for research as they list the locations of all cemeteries in the area.

Dudley Metropolitan Borough Council has a useful search facility on its website at: www.dudley.gov.uk. Under the heading 'deaths, funerals and cremations' is a searchable index of all burials in the borough cemeteries and crematoria from 1900; it does not cover churchyard cemeteries, such as that at St John's, Kates Hill, where William Perry, the 'Tipton Slasher', is buried. Other local councils have details of the locations of facilities, but do not have an index similar to the one at Dudley. There are burial registers held at all four archives, dating back to the early nineteenth century.

The Gravestone Photographic Resource website is an international grave monument directory and another growing and developing resource, with a small number of Staffordshire, Worcestershire and West Midlands entries at present. It can be accessed at: www.gravestonephotos.com. The site has a very simple surname search, enabling you to find an ancestor anywhere in the world and currently there are 344,000 names indexed from 18 countries. You may find burial records on CD-ROM from companies such as www.genfair.co.uk or www.familyhistoryresearch. org. Holy Trinity Church, Amblecote, has a memorial index and maps showing the location of graves available at: www.holytrinityamblecote. org.uk.

Chapter 8

CRIME AND PUNISHMENT

Introduction

The Metropolitan Police was established in London in 1829 and this marked the beginning of the formal policing system in Britain. The arrangements for policing in the Black Country before 1829 are discussed here, and then the development of the system in the region during the nineteenth and twentieth centuries and what conditions were like for police officers. Courts existed in various forms centuries before 1829, as did prisons and gaols, and these are also examined. Advice is given about tracing both criminal and policing ancestors, as well as locating records that will explain ancestors' interaction with the criminal justice system. Juvenile crime and the reformatory system established during the Victorian period are detailed and riots, although previously mentioned, are discussed in more depth.

Before the Police

Before the introduction of police forces the Black Country was overseen by a disparate collection of locally appointed officials. In Dudley, as in other towns, it was the business of the Borough Court Leet to elect officers for the year. In 1732 there were two constables and a serjeant appointed, among others such as 'food testers'. This number of two constables was totally inadequate considering the hundreds of taverns and beer shops in the town. The Court Leet met for the last time in Dudley in 1866.

In 1830s Darlaston there was no magistrate and no courthouse, the nearest court being at Bilston. One man acted as constable, watchman and beadle. The beadle was a parish appointment who kept order in church and also carried out some 'enforcement' functions in the community. In many areas the parish was the only form of local government until the nineteenth century. The parish constable was an Anglo-Saxon/ Norman office, unpaid and elected. If appointed by the parish vestry, service was compulsory. By the nineteenth century it was normal for a citizen to pay a deputy to serve. There is evidence to suggest that in the

Black Country some constables served for a number of years and became 'professional' constables. The 'Watch' was appointed to patrol larger towns especially at night. The table below gives an indication of the development of the watch and police during the nineteenth century.

The Development of the Watch and Police in the Nineteenth Century

Town	Watch	Police Force
Walsall	1811	1832 (3 officers)
Wolverhampton	1814	1837 (12 officers)
Dudley	1816	1840 (9 officers)

Much of the Black Country was covered by the county forces of Staffordshire, which came into being in October 1842, and Worcestershire, which began in 1840. When Dudley Borough was formed in 1888 it qualified to set up its own borough force, however it remained part of Worcestershire Constabulary until 1920.

Jonathan Wild from Wolverhampton was cool, audacious and clever – he knew enough to twist the law to suit his own ends. In the early eighteenth century, before the introduction of police forces, he committed his first crime, when he was offered some stolen goods. Instead of buying them, he contacted their owner anonymously and offered to recover them 'no questions asked'. The deal was accepted and a reward was paid, which was shared between Wild and the thief. Over time Wild organised a team of reliable thieves, making sure that they targeted people he knew could pay a reward for the return of their goods.

Eventually, Wild had to leave Wolverhampton, as suspicions were aroused about his activities. He moved to London, where he already had contacts and could operate on a larger scale. He even branched out to Ostend in Belgium, having accrued enough money to buy a small ship. However, in 1724 Wild was captured with stolen goods onboard, and further investigations uncovered his double life and the extent of his criminal empire. He was tried at the Old Bailey, found guilty and sentenced to death and was hanged at Tyburn. More details on this fascinating character can be found in David J Cox and Michael Pearson's *Foul Deeds and Suspicious Deaths Around the Black Country* (2006).

The 'New' Police

In 1829 policing in England and Wales was radically changed with the introduction of the Metropolitan Police, the first real police force in

Britain. In the years that followed police forces began to be formed in towns and counties across England and Wales. Legislation passed during the mid-nineteenth century enabled and then mandated the creation of police forces. In 1832 the first Walsall Police Force was established and the town clerk wrote to the Commissioner of the Metropolitan Police for a recommendation for who should lead the force. FH West and three other officers were appointed. The total police 'staff' comprised 2 constables appointed at the Court Leet, 2 serjeants at mace, 16 deputy constables for the borough and 20 for the 'foreign'. In 1835 the introduction of the Municipal Corporation Act brought further change. At this time, Walsall was the only 'incorporated' town in the region and the councillors set up a Watch Committee and the cost of maintaining the force fell on the rate payers. West left as a result of a change in his responsibilities. From 1836 to 1838 there were four police officers (a superintendent and three police constables). Walsall Police were provided with a station house, which incorporated two cells for the confinement of prisoners (before appearing at court); these cells were probably in a worse condition than the town gaol. It was normal for prisoners to be held overnight, but some were held for as long as eight days, and in one recorded instance a woman was held for two weeks (*1st Report Commissioners on the Municipal Corporation of England and Wales* (1835)).

After 1836 the Walsall force grew slowly, but a new station was built in 1843, next to the Guildhall in Goodall Street. There were some personnel problems and between 1836 and 1850 there were four changes in super-intendent in the force, and two of these, Superintendent John Rofe and Superintendent Burton, were dismissed by the Watch Committee. John Wyatt Carter of Bath was appointed to the force in 1855. Carter remained in post for thirty years.

John W Childs was a sergeant in Walsall from 1855 to 1886. When he joined there were twelve constables, paid 18s per week, and two sergeants. Officers wore swallow-tailed coats and shiny top hats and carried cutlasses. In 1857, following recommendations from HM Inspector of Constabulary, the size of the force in Walsall was expanded to 1 super-intendent, 4 sergeants and 19 constables. During a miners' strike at Bilston 1,000 miners marched on Walsall looting and emptying market stalls. Childs said that the force formed a line across the miners' route and drew their cutlasses, the miners turned back and did not return. Childs reminisced: 'I have seen fighting all Saturday nights … An Irishman hit me with a large stick on the face and broke two teeth. I thought my head was gone. I could not eat solid food for two months. I have also been shot; my top coat was riddled with shots and five or six entered my body.' (quoted in a pamphlet at Walsall Local History Centre).

Walsall was a tough town to work in, live in and visit. In December 1865 thirty robberies were reported in the borough (not including the foreign). These were a mixture of day, evening and night-time offences and property stolen included cash, watches and a whip! One of the robberies was committed at St Matthew's Church. These were just the incidents that were reported, and the reality of crime in the nineteenth century is similar to that of today, and the number of crimes committed was likely to have been much higher. In the 1860s robbery was a very similar crime to that of today, 'the felonious taking of money or goods, from another, in presence, against his will, by violence or putting him in fear'. Robbery was a crime that led to a fear of the breakdown of law and order. Highway robbery and a spate of garrottings (seizing a victim by the throat to keep him still during the robbery) had caused panic across the country, especially in London.

During the 1860s there were 487 prosecutions for robbery in the Black Country. They included the case of John Rutter, a saddler, who was hit on the head by a life saver and robbed of £1 and a silk handkerchief. For the man who struck the blow the sentence was death, later commuted to seven years' transportation. Robbery is a very personal crime and can include threats or physical contact between offender and victim. Also, in some crimes the amount of violence used far outweighs that needed to facilitate the crime. Again, similar to today, many offences were committed against victims 'worse for drink'. Baron Watson at a Worcestershire Assize Court commented: 'The lower class of people resorted to public houses ... and on coming out at night, some one was followed, knocked down, and robbed'. An analysis of 92 robbers convicted between 1839 and 1860 in Dudley showed that 49 per cent of offenders were miners, 12 per cent were labourers and few had no occupation.

The annual reports of the Walsall Borough Chief Constable are at Walsall Local History Centre, and two volumes cover the period 1890 to 1920. Also there are five volumes of Walsall Watch Committee minutes.

In 1837 Wolverhampton set up its police force at the behest of the town commissioners. They appointed Metropolitan Police Sergeant Richard Castle to head the force. Other Black Country towns waited until 1839 and the introduction of the County Police Act, which allowed magistrates to establish uniformed and paid police officers. Worcestershire adopted the Act for the whole of the county. Staffordshire adopted it for the South Division of the Offlow South Hundred, and this covered much of the area of the Black Country that fell within the county. Staffordshire established a force comprising 1 superintendent, 2 sergeants and 18 constables. In 1842 a police force was created for the whole of the county of Staffordshire. The 'Mining District' was one of three divisions and its headquarters was at West Bromwich. Wolverhampton disbanded its force and merged with Staffordshire as a result of the 1839 County Police Act, but Walsall remained independent because of its incorporated status. A change in local government in Wolverhampton, when it became a municipal borough, enabled it to establish a borough police force, which it did in 1848.

The role of the parish constable remained until 1847 (in Staffordshire) and 1851 (in Worcestershire). A number of the parish constables joined the 'new' forces and their previous experience was valuable. As they were drawn from the community they knew both potential victims and offenders, and this was particularly beneficial in the tight-knit mining villages.

The beginning of central government influence was seen in Wolverhampton in 1855 following riots in the town. This situation required troops to be deployed to support the police, and as a result prompted the Home Office to recommend increasing the size of the police force from 39 to 54. By 1860 the police forces in the Black Country had a combined strength of 262 officers.

In 1870 there were police forces in Walsall (32 officers) and Wolverhampton (69 officers), while Dudley and Halesowen were part of the Worcestershire force, which had a total strength of 189. In 1939 Dudley had a force of 80 men, compared at that time with 120 in Walsall and 170 in Wolverhampton. A useful reference work for policing in Victorian times is David Philips' *Crime and Authority in Victorian England: The Black Country 1835– 1960* (1977). In addition, Clive Emsley's *The English Police* (1996) and *The British Bobby* (2010) are useful in researching policing since 1829.

The most heinous of crimes is, of course, murder. The Black Country has had its fair share of murders throughout history, many of which have been well documented, for example, in Michael Pearson and David Cox's *Foul Deeds and Suspicious Deaths Around the Black Country* (2006). The book includes the dreadful case of the murder of Mary Ann Mason. She was a beautiful young woman who was shot in the face with a cavalry carbine by her jealous boyfriend, Joseph Meadows, who later hanged for his crime. Other interesting titles are Michael Posner's *Midlands Murders* (2010) and Harold Parsons' *Murder and Mystery in the Black Country* (1989).

Bilston police station, now replaced by a modern building nearby. (Author's photograph)

By 1933 there were 164 police forces in England and Wales. However, the Home Office believed that a more acceptable number was nine. The number of forces has reduced significantly to forty-three, including West Midlands, the second largest force in England and Wales. The two main force amalgamations to affect the Black Country took place in 1966 and 1974. In 1966 West Midlands Police was first formed when the county boroughs covering the Black Country were merged, superseding the independent forces in Dudley, Walsall and Wolverhampton. In 1974 West Midlands Police grew to its current size, incorporating Birmingham, Solihull and Coventry.

Life in the Police

Turnover in the police was high, the two major factors being drunkenness and a failure to accept discipline, which was often very harsh. Constables supplied their own boots, and pay was frequently docked almost indiscriminately for matters such as lateness, drinking on duty and swearing. The chief constable had the power to appoint and dismiss, seemingly at will. Hatton, the Chief Constable of Staffordshire, for example, dismissed Sergeant Michael Stewart for misconduct in November 1847 following a corruption investigation at force headquarters in Wolverhampton. Stewart was re-appointed in January 1848, and had risen to superintendent by 1865.

Over many years pay was an issue for police officers, and this continued until 1979, when the Edmund Davis agreement linked police pay to the cost of living. When the new police forces were set up wages were not competitive with those of skilled labourers. Miners always earned more than police officers and so it was only the likes of nailers and chain makers who were likely to be attracted by police wages. In a debate on police pay in 1851 Lord Wrottesley argued for an increase in pay. Basic pay for a constable was 15s, little more than his wagoners were paid. Magistrates agreed that some skilled workers at the time were earning 25–30s a week. The outcome of the debate, however, was that wages should stay the same, and so the 'catchment' base for police officers accordingly remained poorly paid labouring classes. There were times during the twentieth century when officers were eligible to claim state benefits because of low pay.

Many unmarried police officers were required to live in single quarters, often above the police station. Until 1935 there were rooms for twelve officers at Dudley Police Station in Priory Street, with twelve cottages at the rear of the police buildings for married men. In 1935 the cottages were demolished and twelve flats provided at the junction of The Broadway and Tower Street. After the Second World War a new police and fire station were constructed in Tower Street, and this remains the location of Dudley Police Station, although the fire station has moved. The flats were demolished as a result of a dispute about their use and the land became a car park. Basil Bradford's *Dudley Borough Police 1920–1966* (1988) gives an insight into life in Dudley Borough Police.

Patrol methods changed as policing developed, often as a result of manpower availability. The first system in Dudley was the 'Beat Card Patrol System'. Each officer had a fixed pattern, with a list of 'points' or 'meets' at set times. This was replaced in 1932 by 'concentrated foot patrols', still using beats. This was the 'Police Box System', which had no set pattern for patrol, and the box had a telephone linked to the station and officers called in hourly. The officer had total discretion about where to patrol. While this was an efficient patrol method, it isolated officers for almost the whole of their duty.

During the Second World War duties again changed. Officers aged 31 and above were in 'reserved occupations' and could not leave, but officer numbers reduced. New roles were taken on. Coroner's enquiries in

Dudley, for example, were taken on by Basil Bradford because he could drive and type. He recalls a tragic incident one Christmas Eve when a house fire led to the death of four children; the Coroner's verdict was that death was caused by asphyxiation from smoke from burning furniture. Coroner's records are available at local archives, but are closed for seventy-five years.

After the war a more familiar patrol method was adopted, using teams of officers and radios. Sergeants were responsible for designating patrols. The final system came in during the mid-1950s, when a reduced 'box' system was introduced. Wooden boxes were replaced with better equipped brick-built boxes and use was made of lightweight motor-cycles, known as 'Noddy Bikes'. This system remained until the 1966 amalgamations.

The first women to work in the police were called 'Women's Police Volunteers' and 'Women's Patrols', which were formed in 1914 to control the behaviour of young women. These were replaced by the 'Women Police' in 1918. Branches were formed around the country, although the women were not part of the regular police and not able to make arrests. Their principal duties involved women and children. This remained the situation until the 1970s, when women were fully integrated in police forces and constabularies around the country. The first two women police in the Black Country were recruited in Walsall in 1918.

Policing Records

Policing records are complicated because of the number of amalgama-tions of forces throughout the existence of the police. The most recent amalgamations took place in 1974 with the formation of the West Midlands Police, which now polices the whole of the Black Country. A online search on 'police' at: www.blackcountryhistory.org reveals many photographs of both officers and police stations, chief constable report books, public office books, expenditure reports, case reports and docu-ments on police social activities. Useful publications include Martin Stallion and David S Wall's *The British Police: Police Forces and Chief Officers 1829–2012* (2012) and Stephen Wade's *Tracing Your Criminal Ancestors* (2009). The Police History Society website at: www.policehistorysociety. co.uk gives a good overview of policing and features useful links. Also, West Midlands Police have a museum and the website at: www.west midlandspolicemuseum.co.uk describes the history and development of policing in the Black Country, gives useful genealogical advice and the opening hours and holdings of the museum.

Punishment Through the Ages

The Courts and Prisons

Before 1972 there were three types of courts in England. The lower courts were the Petty Sessions or Magistrates Courts, also known as Police Courts. These still operate today, either as a panel of three magistrates or a single magistrate sitting alone, called a District Judge. These deal with summary (less serious) offences. Magistrates are drawn from the local community and the office dates from the 1300s. Until 1972 there were two higher courts. The Quarter Sessions met quarterly in each county and county borough from 1388 onwards. The Courts of Assize sat periodically and heard the most serious of cases, committed to the Assize Court by the Quarter Sessions. In 1972 these two courts were replaced by the Crown Courts. For crimes committed in the Black Country serious cases would have been heard at either Stafford or Worcester Assizes and, if found guilty, stiffer sentences were usually handed out at the Assizes. The Assize Courts were paid for by central government, Quarter Sessions by the county, so there were examples of cases being sent to the Assizes to save money for the county.

When searching records it is important to note that there is a difference between a 'convict' and a 'prisoner'. A convict was given a substantial sentence, for example transportation, death or a long period of hard labour. A prisoner could have been a debtor or someone awaiting trial. The best source of information for court and crime proceedings is probably newspapers, which often give verbatim accounts of trials and a lot of coverage of crime. Newspapers can be researched on the website of the British Newspaper Archive at: www.britishnewspaperarchive.co.uk.

Assize Courts

During the nineteenth and twentieth centuries six circuits comprised the Assize Courts around England. Court cases for offences committed in the Black Country were heard by judges on the Oxford Circuit. Generally, Assize judges visited each circuit twice a year, usually in February/March and again in July/August. They dealt with the most serious cases, as well as some civil cases that may be of interest to family historians.

As today, in the mid-nineteenth century committals to the Assize Courts were overwhelmingly for property offences – almost 80 per cent of cases between 1836 and 1860 fell into this category. Public order offences fluctuated, depending on environmental circumstances. In 1842, for example, high unemployment led to strikes and riots which in turn caused an increase in public-order cases. Court sentences were more severe than today and during the mid-nineteenth century the common sentence for a first conviction for larceny (theft) was imprisonment, while a second or third conviction could result in transportation, as could any suggestion that an offender was 'hardened' or 'persistent'. Transportation for ten years usually meant transportation to Australia, while a transportation sentence of seven years meant the convict was held in a prison hulk and never actually left the country. The death penalty by this time was normally reserved for murder convictions and between 1835 and 1860 the death sentence was carried out four times in the Black Country. Serious crimes, such as rape, wounding or robbery, may have attracted the death penalty, but this was routinely commuted to transportation or later, penal servitude.

Useful records include gaol delivery calendars, giving prisoner names, place and date of the Assize Court and any sentence imposed. The indictment, normally compiled by the Clerk of the Assize, is also helpful as it contains a description of the accused, his address and victim details. However, there are gaps in the records held, especially before 1650, and locally not all records have survived. TNA has extensive holdings including registers or calendars of prisoners and criminal registers. Ancestry has a very useful index of 1.4 million trials between 1791 and 1892 and this can be viewed online at: http://search.ancestry.co.uk/search/db.aspx?dbid=1590.

Local newspapers often printed Assize Court lists as well as Quarter Session case lists. For Worcestershire, *Berrows Worcester Journal* lists were often found among other items of news including births, deaths and marriages. *Worcester Herald* and *Wolverhampton Chronicle* also reported cases.

Quarter Sessions

Justice often seemed very harsh, given the miserable conditions many people lived in:

> I go to pick at the pitheaps. It's the only way I can get fuel to keep me from starving these cold nights ... There were two poor creatures committed to Stafford Gaol last week for stealing coal, and they were only just picking out a few bits from what the pit people threw away for rubbish.

Between 1827 and 1855 all such larcenies had to be prosecuted on indictment at Quarter Sessions. Juries were often warned not to discharge prisoners on the basis they had only stolen a small amount of coal or iron.

Warwickshire County Record Office has a useful online database of Calendars of Prisoners (1800–1900) on its website at: www.warwickshire. gov.uk/countyrecordoffice. This allows you to search for individual accused and victims, across both Assize and Quarter Session records. There are gaps in the records and some have not survived. A photo-copy of the original record can be ordered by contacting the record office. Some Black Country towns are included, for example, Darlaston, Wednesbury and West Bromwich. It is also possible that among the list of names there may be someone of interest to you who 'strayed' into Warwickshire and was either arrested or a victim of crime. One further resource from TNA is a guide to criminals in the eighteenth, nineteenth and twentieth centuries at: http://tinyurl.com/atko4.

Local archives hold records of Quarter Sessions, County Court papers, Petty Sessions and Coroners Court records. It is worth noting that most are subject to the thirty-year rule, except Coroner's records, which are closed for seventy-five years.

Magistracy
In the second quarter of the nineteenth century, the magistracy in the Black Country was dominated by industrialists rather than landowners. This change was accompanied by increased prosecutions for industrial theft, which rose markedly between 1835 (10 per cent of cases) and 1860 (33 per cent of cases). During this period it also became easier to try people summarily for petty offences, leading to an increase in cases. Drink-related crimes were also routinely dealt with by magistrates.

In 1880 Brierley Hill had a Magistrates Court and stealing from the colliery was a common crime at this time, mainly during winter months, although serious crimes were unusual, as was vandalism. There were two sittings a week. In January 1880 one case reported in local newspapers was that of James Thompson, a local tramp. Thompson was sentenced to one month's hard labour for destroying his clothing. He was resident at the workhouse at Wordsley and claimed he was ashamed of his clothes, which is why he destroyed them. There had, at this time, been an 'epidemic' of similar cases in Dudley Workhouse.

A selection of drink-related cases was heard at Brierley Hill on 15 January 1880. Chain maker Albert Billingham was fined 5s for being 'drunk and wanting to fight' at Quarry Bank; night soil man Thomas Jones was fined 2s 6d for being 'drunk and incapable'; Lot Billingham, described as 'a respectably dressed youth' aged 17 years, was fined 10s for being drunk and using 'very obscene language'; and, finally, collier

Edward Worrall was found on the ground drunk and had to be taken home, and was fined 5s (or seven days' hard labour).

Poaching was dealt with rigorously by the courts, as evidenced by the case of James Blackshaw at Brierley Hill in 1880. James was described as 'a respectable looking man' and a glass worker. He was found by a policeman with a pheasant in his pocket. Blackshaw explained that the Earl of Stamford and Warrington was out shooting with friends on his Enville Estate and that he, Blackshaw, had just happened to be there. He said he had found the pheasant, which was wounded, and killed it and that he was going home to eat it for dinner. Blackshaw was fined 5s and costs for 'trespassing in pursuit of gain'.

Useful reference books include David T Hawkings' *Criminal Ancestors* (2009) and Stephen Wade's *Tracing Your Criminal Ancestors* (2009). There are plenty of magistrates' records at the archives and these include magistrates' notebooks, court registers and licensing registers (for public houses).

Juvenile Crime

Until 1854 child convicts and prisoners were treated in the same way as adults. From 1838 many young convicts were sent to Parkhurst Prison. In 1854 Parliament passed the Youthful Offenders Acts to try and combat the problem of children who had been neglected or abandoned and had turned to crime. The Act authorised the establishment of reformatories and industrial schools with Treasury grants. Children under 16 found guilty of a criminal offence could be sent to reformatories for between two and five years, following a prison sentence of at least fourteen days. Industrial schools were intended to catch children at a younger age and children between 7 and 14 could be sent to one for any period up to their 15th birthday for committing a crime under the age of 12, for begging, being destitute or out of parental control.

By 1865, fifty-two reformatories and thirty-three industrial schools existed in England and Wales. There were no reformatories located in the Black Country, and the nearest ones were in Birmingham, at Saltley, Harbourne, Witton and Sparkbrook. There was only one industrial school in Wolverhampton, but this was little more than a truant school and was not residential. The Missing Ancestors website at: www.missing-ancestors.com features a list of industrial and reform schools, as well as some ragged schools. The list is not complete, but work is on-going and there are census extracts for some schools. One of the inmates at Birmingham Free Industrial School, for example, in 1891 was 14-year-old John Attwood from Oldbury. Black Country children were often sent all over the country to reformatories, and regular destinations were Liverpool, Manchester and Leeds.

There was a major 'youth' problem in the Black Country in the nineteenth century. In 1875 the Wolverhampton Watch Committee reported a 'gang of 40 thieves who were a menace and a plague to the town'. Most juvenile crime amounted to petty larceny, which would most probably be labelled as 'shoplifting' today. Pawnbrokers were seen as contributing to the 'epidemic' as they often took items from young children. This was despite a law passed in 1872 making it illegal to take items from children under 12. Don Cochrane's *Black Country Criminal Ancestors 1787–1868* (2003) includes plenty of examples of cases heard at both the Assizes and County Sessions. In the Worcester Assizes in 1835, for example, Benjamin Bingham (aged 18) and Sarah Wheeler (aged 19) were convicted of stealing property including a fowl and a horse and received transportation for seven years. In the same case Hyla Holden (aged 17) was convicted of receiving the fowl and was transported for fourteen years.

Magistrates generally blamed parents for the wrongdoings of their children, and there was evidence that parents actively encouraged their children to steal. However, much of the theft was a result of poverty and the struggle to survive. In 1879 many families were refused outdoor relief and would not enter the workhouse and as a consequence theft was commonplace. Dudley Magistrates, in March 1887, reported, 'Within the past 6 months, there have been 42 children charged with serious offences – a few bad boys were running about the streets corrupting the whole town'. By the 1890s, the authorities began to deal with the problem of juvenile behaviour generally, rather than simply concentrating on larceny.

Wolverhampton Archives and Local Studies Service has a series of reports on reformatories and industrial schools around the country, and these cover annual inspections and financial and statistical data. To find possible ancestors detained under the reformatory system it is necessary to contact the relevant archive where a reformatory was located. Liverpool, for example, has a number of records relating to local reformatories and there is a searchable index. Documents include a roll of juvenile offenders from 1890–1904, with details of who the detainee was chargeable to. To view records themselves it is necessary to visit the archive itself.

Findmypast have recently added a number of Manchester Prison Registers to their online resources at: www.findmypast.co.uk/search/manchester-collection. These cover the period from 1847–1881, and industrial school records from 1866–1912.

Prison and Gaol

Prior to Victorian times prison was not used for long-term sentences and death, transportation or flogging were the more usual outcomes. During the last two decades of the eighteenth century there was a boom in prison building, partly because it was no longer possible to transport convicts to America. National reform of prisons began in 1823 with the Gaol Act. As a result, running prisons for profit was abolished and inspection on a quarterly basis was introduced. The subsequent reports were sent to the Home Secretary. In 1835 five Inspectors of Prisons were appointed and reported to central government, but had no enforcement powers. In 1844 there was further reform and new prisons were constructed to implement the 'separate' system, long-term solitary confinement for most of the day. The Prison Commission was established by the 1877 Prison Act and the Home Office then took over responsibility for the system.

Female prisoners were guarded by female warders. In the mid-eighteenth century about one in five prisoners was a woman, and their sentences tended to be shorter than for men and rehabilitation was seen as having a good chance of success. As there were fewer women prisoners there was more opportunity for them to be treated as individuals. Lady visitors were encouraged to help to reform women.

Prison officers in male prisons were strictly regulated and talking to prisoners was forbidden, as was speaking to colleagues while on duty. The service had a paramilitary structure and drew many of its recruits from the armed services. Pay was poor, leading to possible exposure to temptation and corruption.

Today the terms 'prison' and 'gaol' (or jail) are interchangeable. The main difference in the past was that a gaol was a local facility for housing prisoners who might be awaiting trial and a prison was a state facility where prisoners were sent to serve their sentence. One surviving example of an early gaol is in Derby and it now operates as a museum. The museum's website gives visiting details and background history relating to gaols in general at: www.derbygaol.com. There were a number of gaols located in the Black Country, one of which was in Walsall. In 1802 the gaol comprised two rooms under the town hall, and later was extended to six, still inadequate, cells. In that year William Mason was the gaoler and although he was not paid a salary, he received a sum of money for each detained person. The cell for felons was little more than a dungeon. It had iron-grated windows (no glass) and straw for bedding and food and water were passed through the grating. The magistrates were supposed to inspect the gaol, but the gaoler stated he had never known them to visit during the winter.

A somewhat more comfortable facility existed in Wolverhampton. It was re-built in 1800 and its gaoler George Roberts was paid an annual salary of 80s. Male and female prisoners had separate facilities. The men had a dayroom with a fireplace, a work room and two solitary cells. There were ten sleeping cells and an infirmary room. Women had a day room and a work room and their cells had rush mattresses with blankets. In a report Wolverhampton Gaol was described as 'clean and the cells well-ventilated'. A helpful reference work is Trevor May's *Victorian and Edwardian Prisons* (2006). The nineteenth-century Calendar of Prisoners available from Ancestry also contains useful information.

Transportation and Prison

From the early seventeenth century transportation was frequently used for people convicted of crimes, and even those guilty of minor theft were dealt with in this way. Up until the 1770s as many as 50,000 convicts are estimated to have been transported to the Americas, but this stopped with the American War of Independence. From this time until 1868 Australia was the destination for those sentenced to transportation. The last convict ship arrived in Western Australia in 1868. TNA has convict records in its collection HO 11, and these are also available from Ancestry. A free list of those transported to Australia can be found at: www.slq.qld.gov.au/info/fh/convicts. In 1787 the 'first fleet', comprising eleven ships, set sail for Australia to establish a penal colony and arrived in January 1788. Prior to their being transported, convicts were held in gaol, but when these became overcrowded prison hulks were used.

Local prisons for the Black Country were Winson Green (Birmingham), Stafford and Worcester. Apart from visiting the prison chapel and exercise, prisoners were kept in their cells, where they worked, slept and ate. They were provided with a Bible, a prayer book and eating utensils. Food in prison was not pleasant. Bread and gruel were given to short-term prisoners, serving up to one week, and as the sentence increased the quality and quantity of food improved. Work, as distinguished from hard labour, was not always meant to be productive. Picking oakum was a good source of income for some prisons. After trade unions complained about unfair competition for their members, prisoners were restricted to producing mailbags and prison uniforms from the oakum through this activity. Prisoners also carried out repair work on the prison.

Career details of prison staff are likely to be found in visiting committee minutes, together with salary and other information. Prison records were not kept in a uniform manner, so information kept differs from prison to prison and not all records have survived.

Habitual criminals registers are useful as they have prisoner details and a photograph, and were started nationwide in 1805. For much of England they are digitised at Ancestry. Wolverhampton Archive and Local Studies Service also holds habitual drunkard registers. Prisoners can be found on census returns, so if an ancestor's name is absent it is worth checking if it is recorded in places like Dartmoor and Winson Green. In the nineteenth century many convicts were housed on one of the nineteen prison ships berthed in British harbours. Ancestry also holds prison hulk registers from 1802–49.

Riots

Riot and rebellion is sometimes seen as a modern phenomenon, but this is not the case. Throughout history people have rioted, usually as a reaction to events that have affected their lives. Before the Restoration of the monarchy in 1660 keeping the peace was a problem and watchmen, constables and men sworn in as special constables were the first response in situations. If this did not resolve matters, then the military had to be deployed. This task often fell to the local yeomanry or militia, but after the Restoration a small standing army was in place and it was often used by magistrates to quell riots. This was not popular with the people, and there is evidence that the military were also unhappy being deployed in this way.

Riots were sometimes the only way the populace, or a sector of it, could express their views. Until the twentieth century most people were not given the vote, and the class system meant the working class had little representation in decision-making forums and they were not consulted on matters that had a major impact on their lives. In the eighteenth century food riots were common and the political situation also caused unrest. In 1750 Jacobite riots in Walsall, Wednesbury and Birmingham lasted intermittently for two months. Ian Gilmour's *Riots, Risings and Revolution* (1993), which examines governance and violence in eighteenth-century England, is very useful and is available from Amazon as an eBook.

In 1835 there were election riots in Wolverhampton. One of the local magistrates, John Clare, swore in a number of special constables to deal with the disturbances in the town. He then decided that it was necessary to call in the military and thirty-two Dragoon Guards were despatched from Dudley to assist, followed by a troop of horse from Stourbridge. Another magistrate, Henry Hill, removed himself to his house and despite

163

letters imploring him to return to the town, he did not become involved in the situation until much later, at 11pm. Once the Riot Act had been read the Dragoons charged the crowd and three people were shot, one of whom had to have his leg amputated, while others were struck by cavalry sabres. After the riots an enquiry was held and the need to call in the military was questioned. As the only damage caused during the 'riot' appeared to be four broken windows, concern was also expressed about the heavy-handed approach of the Dragoons. One (unnamed) letter-writer said: 'Decrepit old men, and even women, did not escape their [the Dragoons'] fury, but were savagely beaten and cut down by the ferocious soldiery'. One of those writing about their concerns was Henry Hill, who appears to have been a sensible and experienced magistrate. Once he arrived at the scene he took control of the military and the special constables, and went about closing public houses and dispersing crowds, without direct intervention of military personnel. The upshot was that by 2am the following morning peace had been restored.

The enquiry exonerated the Dragoons, and even went as far as congratulating them on their work that night. There was mention of the death of one of the Dragoon horses during the disturbances. A post-mortem was held and it was found that it had probably died from a heart attack. An injury to the horse was thought to have been caused during its fall to the ground. This received more attention during the enquiry than the serious injuries caused to townspeople. Hansard provides a useful transcript of proceedings in the House of Commons when these riots were debated, and this can be found online at: http://hansard.millbank systems.com/commons/1835/jun/01/disturbance-at-wolverhampton.

Nailers in the Black Country had an unfortunate time in 1842. Tommy shop prices for goods that nailers had to buy were 30–40 per cent higher than regular shops, and they were threatened with dismissal if they refused to accept the truck system. Most nailers could not earn more than 4s 6d per week, and most of this was spent on rent, fuel and tools, with little left for food. In April the nail masters reduced the wages of the nailers by 20 per cent and this led to strikes and rioting in Dudley and elsewhere on Monday 25 April. The Birmingham correspondent of *The Times* wrote, 'on Monday morning some thousands of workmen congregated from Lye Waste, Cradley, Rowley and Netherton and proceeded to visit the works of several of the most extensive and influential masters of this populous manufacturing district'. Some prominent nail masters, such as Mr Nock of Cradley Heath, Joseph Jones of Reddall Hill and Mr Lewis of Darby Hand, were seized by nailers and marched to Dudley. They were taken to confront other masters. Burgess, Chief

Commissioner of Police in Birmingham, sent fifty police officers to Dudley. Military forces were also deployed in the form of a troop of Enniskillen Dragoons. About forty prisoners were captured by the military.

The situation was very tense until Wednesday when a company of artillery was despatched to Dudley and further troops stationed at Halesowen and Oldbury. Police arrested a number of ringleaders, including Benjamin Bache, who would later be sentenced to four months' hard labour for his part in the riots.

The strikes and disorder spread to the mining industry, and Rowley Regis and West Bromwich were both affected. There were also problems in Staffordshire, Norton Canes and the Potteries. In October 1842, at Stafford, a special commission was held to try the 274 rioters arrested from across the Black Country and Staffordshire. As a result, five men were transported for life following a serious assault on Benjamin Benton, sworn in as a special constable at Bilston and stationed at Walbutt's Colliery. Benton was recognised by a mob as someone who had helped detain rioters the previous night. He was pursued and severely beaten and cut by the mob. On passing sentence, Mr Baron Rolfe said, 'You have been convicted of felony, which has disclosed a painful and melancholy scene of turbulence and disaffection rarely known ... I would feel myself wanting in the discharge of my duty if I did not pronounce you to be severally transported beyond the seas for the term of your natural lives'. Other prisoners received varying sentences of hard labour and those charged with minor offences were acquitted, having served two months awaiting trial. Arthur Willetts' *The Black Country Nailer's Riots of 1842* (1995) provides plenty of information on this episode and relevant material can also be found at TNA in series HO 42 and HO 17.

Chapter 9

ARCHIVES AND RESOURCES

Main Archives

There are four archives covering the Black Country: Dudley, Smethwick, Walsall and Wolverhampton. In addition, material at Stafford and Worcester archives may be of use. Stourbridge Library, a satellite of Dudley, holds many records for that town. All main archives hold birth, marriage, death and census records, parish and other church registers, maps and photographs, local-authority records (school records, rate books and electoral registers), Poor Law records and local newspapers.

You will need a CARN reader's ticket to use the services, and this is easily obtained on your first visit to an archive by taking two forms of identification with you. The CARN ticket is free of charge. Many records will be accessed on microfiche or microfilm, and pre-booking of a reader is essential to access these records.

The first visit to an archive may be daunting and there are things you can do to make it more productive. Many archives have websites and these usually list what is available so some planning can be done in advance. On arrival, staff will do their best to assist you, often suggesting lines of research using material contained within their archive, and explain the rules.

Dudley
Dudley Archives and Local History Services
Mount Pleasant Street
Coseley
WV14 9JR
Tel/fax: 01384 812770
Website: www.dudley.gov.uk/archives

Covers the whole of the Borough of Dudley, including Halesowen, Cradley, Pedmore, Stourbridge, Lye, Brierley Hill, Gornal, Kingswinford, Sedgley and Coseley. Some material relating to Cradley Heath and South Staffordshire (especially Himley). Records specific to Dudley include

Earls of Dudley estate records, business records and much more. Free Internet access is available, with access to Ancestry (pre-booking advised for this).

Sandwell
Sandwell Community History and Archives Service
Smethwick Library
High Street
Smethwick
B66 1AA
Tel: 01215 582561
Fax: 01215 556064
Website: www.sandwell.gov.uk/archives
Email: archives_service@Sandwell.gov.uk

Covers the whole of the borough of Sandwell, including Oldbury, Rowley Regis, Smethwick, Tipton, Wednesbury and West Bromwich. Sandwell has documents dating back to September 1369, the oldest item being a deed of John Wilkys of Darlaston.

Walsall
Walsall Local History Centre
Essex Street
Walsall
WS2 7AS
Tel: 01922 721305
Fax: 01922 634954
Website: www.walsall.gov.uk/localhistorycentre
Email: localhistorycentre@walsall.gov.uk

Located in the town centre and covers Walsall Metropolitan Borough, including Aldridge, Bloxwich, Brownhills, Darlaston and Willenhall.

Wolverhampton
Wolverhampton Archives and Local Studies Service
Molineux Hotel Building
Whitmore Hill
Wolverhampton
WV1 1SF
Tel: 01902 552480
Fax: 01902 552481

Walsall Local History Centre. (Author's photograph)

Website: www.wolverhampton.gov.uk/archives
Email: archives@wolverhampton.gov.uk

Originally built in the mid-eighteenth century, this building is probably one of the most impressive archive buildings in the area. It was restored in 2003 following a fire and many of the original historic interiors have been re-created in the Georgian style.

Stafford
Staffordshire Record Office
Eastgate Street
Stafford
ST16 2LZ
Tel: 01785 278379
Fax: 01785 278384
Website: www.staffordshire.gov.uk/leisure/archives/homepage.aspx
Email: staffordshire.record.office@staffordshire.gov.ukStafford

Records here relate to the northern part of the Black Country.

Worcester
Worcester County Record Office
The Hives
Sawmill Walk
The Butts
Worcester
WR1 3NZ
Tel: 01905 765922/765924
Fax: 01905 765925
Website: www.worcestershire.gov.uk/cms/records.aspx
Email: WLHC@worcestershire.gov

Holds many records relating to Dudley, Halesowen, Pensnett, Stourbridge and areas in the south and west of the Black Country.

Museums and Archives

Some of the museums in the Black Country have their own records and archives which are available to researchers.

Apedale Heritage Centre
Loomer Road
Chesterton,
Newcastle-under-Lyme
Staffordshire
ST5 7JS
Tel/fax: 01782 565050
Website: www.apedale.co.uk
Email: info@apedale.co.uk

Bantock House Museum and Park
Finchfield Road
Wolverhampton
WV3 9LQ
Tel: 01902 552195
Website: www.wolverhamptonart.org.uk
Email: bantockhouse@wolverhampton.org.uk

Explore the period setting of the Bantock family home and discover the stories of the people who lived there. A wide range of exhibitions, events and activities are organised here throughout the year.

Bantock House Museum. (Author's photograph)

Black Country Living Museum
Tipton Road
Dudley
DY1 4SQ
Tel: 01215 579643
Website: www.bclm.co.uk
Email: info@bclm.co.uk

Provides a snapshot of working life in the nineteenth and early twentieth centuries, with houses, school, mine, trams, trolleybuses and many other exhibits. Historic buildings from around the Black Country have been moved and rebuilt here to create a record of the traditional skills and enterprise of the people that once lived in the heart of industrial Britain.

Broadfield House Glass Museum
Compton Drive
Kingswinford
Dudley
DY6 9NS
Tel: 01384 812745

Website: www.dudley.gov.uk/leisure-and-culture/museums–galleries/
glass-museum
Email: glass.museum@dudley.gov.uk

Holds an extensive archive collection relating to local and British glass. The museum collects pattern books, catalogues, description books, invoices and other paperwork, as well as photographs of factories, workers and their families. Videos and films of glass making are also collected and some are available for visitors to watch. The museum is the only one in Britain to hold the entire microfiche record of glass pattern books of the Corning Museum of Glass in New York. Material can be viewed on microfiche by appointment.

Dudley Canal Trust
The Car Park (A4123 at Birmingham New Road)
Dudley
DY1 4SB
Tel: 01384 236275
Fax: 01384 456615
Website: www.dudleycanaltrust.org.uk
Email: info@dudleycanaltrust.org.uk

Located adjacent to the BCLM, the trust is dedicated to running canal-boat trips into the famous limestone mines beneath the BCLM. It also has a conservation role.

Dudley Museum and Art Gallery
St James's Road
Dudley
DY1 1HU
Tel: 01384 815575
Website: www.dudley.gov.uk/leisure-and-culture/museums–galleries/
dudley-museum–art-gallery
Email: Dudley.museum@dudley.gov.uk

Himley Hall
Himley Park
Dudley
DY3 4DF
Tel: 01384 817817

Dudley Museum. (Author's photograph)

Website: http://www.dudley.gov.uk/leisure-and-culture/parks-and-open-spaces/himley-hall
Email: Himley.hall@dudley.gov.uk

This great Palladian mansion, located between Kingswinford and Wombourne, was built in the eighteenth century on the site of a medieval manor house belonging to the Earl of Dudley.

The 180 acres of grounds were designed by Capability Brown to include a great lake fed by a series of waterfalls from a higher chain of smaller pools.

National Coalmining Museum
New Road
Overton
Wakefield
WF4 4RH
Tel: 01924 848806
Website: www.ncm.org.uk
Email: info@ncm.org.uk

The Oak House Museum
Oak Road
West Bromwich
B70 8HJ
Tel: 01215 530759
Website: www.sandwell.gov.uk/oakhouse

Red House Glass Cone
High Street
Wordsley
Stourbridge
DY8 4AZ
Tel: 01384 812750
Website: www.dudley.gov.uk/leisure-and-culture/museums–galleries/
red-house-glass-cone
Email: redhouse.cone@dudley.gov.uk

The Redhouse Cone dates from 1788 and is useful to visit in conjunction
with Broadfield House Museum if you have ancestors with glass-working
connections. A free audio tour is available. There are also glass-making
demonstrations, temporary exhibitions and craft studios.

Walsall Leather Museum
Leather Museum
Littleton Street West
Walsall
WS2 8EQ
Tel: 01922 721153
Fax: 01922 725827
Website: www.walsall.gov.uk/leathermuseum
Email: leathermuseum@walsall.gov.uk

The museum is housed in a former leather factory. Car parking is
directly opposite the museum (pay and display) which also has a cafe
and shop.

Walsall Museum and Art Gallery
Lichfield Street
Walsall
WS1 1TR
Tel: 01922 653116
Fax: 01922 632824

Website: www.walsall.gov.uk/index/leisure_and_culture/museums/
walsall_museum.htm
Email: museum@walsall.gov.uk

The museum is located on the first and third floors of Walsall Central
Library, a short walk from both bus and train stations.

Wednesbury Museum and Art Gallery
Holyhead Road
Wednesbury
WS10 7DF
Tel: 01215 560683
Website: www.sandwell.gov.uk/info/200070/museums_and_galleries/
13/wednesbury_museum_and_art_gallery/2

Wightwick Manor and Gardens
Wightwick Bank
Wolverhampton
WV6 8EE
Tel: 01902 761400
Website: www.nationaltrust.org.uk/main/w-wightwickmanor
Email: wightwickmanor@nationaltrust.org.uk

Wightwick Manor. (Author's photograph)

Wightwick is a National Trust property, originally the home of Theodore Mander and later his son Geoffrey. It is a unique house with a special charm; the garden is one of the last to be designed by Thomas Mawson.

Libraries

Only the libraries with material relevant to family history researchers are listed here.

Stourbridge Library
Crown Centre
Stourbridge
DY8 1YE
Tel: 01384 812949 (reference section)
Fax: 01384 812946
Website: www.dudley.gov.uk/leisure-and-culture/libraries/find-a-library/stourbridge-library
Email: stourbridge.library@dudley.gov.uk

There is plenty of archive-related material as part of Dudley Archives: newspapers such as the *County Express* and *Stourbridge News* on microfiche, parish registers, pauper records, maps and books on a wide variety of subjects. There is also an indexed photographic collection and comprehensive subject index similar to that kept by Dudley Archives.

William Salt Library
Eastgate Street
Stafford
ST16 2LZ
Tel: 01785 278372
Fax: 01785 278414
Website: www.staffordshire.gov.uk/leisure/archives/williamsalt/
Email: william.salt.library@staffordshire.gov.uk

Stafford railway station is 10 minutes' walk. No appointment is necessary when visiting but there is limited space available in the reading rooms, so contact the library in advance to ensure they hold the records you require and that they can accommodate you.

There are huge collections of printed books, pamphlets, manuscripts, drawings, watercolours and transcripts. The library continues to collect and preserve books, printed ephemera, pamphlets and illustrative material relating to Staffordshire for present and future generations.

Family History Societies

The Birmingham and Midland Society for Genealogy and Heraldry
Tel: 01562 743912
Website: http://bmsgh.org/index.html
Email: gensec@bmsgh.org

Established in 1963, the society covers the counties of Worcestershire, Staffordshire and Warwickshire and the whole of the Black Country. Local branches are at Wolverhampton and Stourbridge. The website has many contact details and membership includes a quarterly magazine, *Midland Ancestor*.

Sandwell Family History Society
Website: http://sandwellfamilyhistory.co.uk
Email: gffrywbb@aol.com

The society began in 1999 and meets monthly at Hilltop Community Centre.

Walsall Family History Group
Website: http://myweb.tiscali.co.uk/group

Founded in 1981, the group meets on a monthly basis at St Matthew's Community Centre, Walsall.

Local History Groups and Societies

Black Country Society
Website: www.blackcountrysociety.co.uk
Email: editor@blackcountrysociety.co.uk

Founded in 1967 by enthusiasts who felt the Black Country did not receive its fair share of recognition. The society's aim is 'to foster interest in the past, present and future of the Black Country'. At a meeting in October 1968, it called for the establishment of a local industrial museum. Since the establishment of the BCLM, the society and members have continually supported it. The society has a reputation for publishing books and magazines on Black Country subjects, together with an active and varied programme of talks, walks and trips throughout the year. There are branches at Kingswinford and the BCLM, as well as an industrial archaeology section. The two most visible products of the society are its website and quarterly magazine, *Blackcountryman*. The website has articles on a wide range of subjects. There have been thousands of articles published in over 175 issues of the magazine and it contains useful web addresses, information on events and developments in both local and family history. Many back issues are still available for sale and there is a programme under way to digitise older issues.

Amblecote History Society
Website: www.amblecotehistorysociety.org.uk

Meets at the Church Hall, Vicarage Road, Amblecote.

Sedgley Local History Society
Website: www.sedgleylocalhistory.org.uk/sed/tiptonst.html
Email: sedgleylhs@hotmail.com

Formed in 1984 and meets monthly at St Andrew's Church, Bilston Street.

Tipton Local History Group
Tel: 01215 571796
Email: robert_hazel@sandwell.gov.uk

Meets regularly at Tipton Library.

Willenhall Local History Society
Website: www.shercliff.demon.co.uk/whs2008
Email: willenhallhistory@gmail.com

Meets monthly at Willenhall Chart Centre, with a variety of speakers.

History of Wollaston Group
Website: www.historyofwollaston.info

General Websites

Search archives across the Black Country – www.blackcountryhistory.org

Freemasons at the Library and Museum of Freemasonry – www.free-masonry.london.museum

British Newspaper Archive – www.britishnewspaperarchive.co.uk

Postal heritage, a history of postal services and Royal Mail Group war memorials, including those in the Black Country, images of post boxes made in the Black Country, oral histories and much more – www. postalheritage.org.uk

Blacksheep index includes police reports on crime, police records, mining and railway indexes – www.blacksheep.co.uk.

Old maps can be examined online, free access to full-resolution maps dating to 1805, possible to compare an area over a series of time periods with a single click – www.old-maps.co.uk

Access to Archives, holds the records of items held in over 400 record offices and other repositories across the country – www.a2a.org.uk.

Appendix 1

MILITARY RECORDS

T his appendix gives a brief insight into how and where you can research military ancestors. It is most likely that an ancestor served in the Army, but information is also provided about locating Royal Navy and Royal Air Force ancestors. In addition, there is some guidance about Home Guard ancestors. The focus is local regiments and units, but people did join regiments outside the Midlands, especially during the world wars.

Army

There was no standing army in England until the mid-1700s. Records of soldiers began to be kept from the late seventeenth century, when the first permanent regiments were formed. The forerunner of the Stafford-shire Regiment was the 38th Foot, which was raised at Lichfield in 1705. The 29th (Worcestershire) Regiment of Foot was formed in 1694 and the Royal Warwickshire Fusiliers in about 1674. There are biographical details for the three most local regiments on the Wikipedia website at: http://en.wikipedia.org/wiki/Main_Page. By the 1880s a structure for the Army was in place and this lasted for eighty years. Recruitment was largely locally based, but not exclusively and officers were commissioned from the middle and upper classes. Soldiers were described by Wellington as the 'dregs of the earth', but he believed they were the best soldiers in the world.

There are many records for Army personnel at TNA, and for officers there are also many regimental archives and written records that have survived. The main collection is WO 97 at TNA, and there is a card index at Kew, but this is also being added to their online catalogue. The only records for soldiers in this collection are for those who survived to receive a pension. They show when and where enlisted, personal descriptions, why they were discharged, where they served, promotion or demotion and details of wives and children. The website Findmypast also has many of these records.

The Church of Latter-Day Saints has filmed *Army Lists* and these are available at their Family History Centres; details can be found at: www.familysearch.org. The online subscription sites, for example, Findmypast, also have a few *Army Lists* in their collections. S&N Genealogical Supplies at: www.genealogysupplies.com/index.php has many *Army* (and *Navy*) *Lists* for sale on CD-ROM. Coverage extends from 1789 and they are mainly useful for officers, but there is also some information regarding militia (infantry) and yeomanry (cavalry) part-time soldiers, as well as regular soldiers. The CD-ROM of the Militia Muster Roll (1781–2) covers a number of counties including Staffordshire, Warwickshire, Worcestershire and Shropshire. These records list the men left in England in the home militia while the regular Army was posted overseas. At TNA there are a range of guides covering military records, and while only a small proportion of these records are available online, they can be viewed at TNA.

There are two useful books about the South Staffordshire Regiment: James P Jones' *History of the South Staffordshire Regiment* (1923), which covers the period from 1707–1923, and Colonel WL Vale's *History of the South Staffordshire Regiment* (1969). There are a number of books documenting the history of the Worcestershire Regiment, for example, HF Stacke's *Worcestershire Regiment in the Great War* (2002), which covers the First World War. Amazon features a number of titles on the regiment on its website, including long out of print books.

Medals are another area worthy of research. You may have medals from one or more of your ancestors, for example, I have my Grandfather's Second World War medals on display at home. However, you may not have the medals, but wish to find out what an ancestor was entitled to receive or simply to know what campaigns he served in. The three categories of medal are gallantry, campaign and long service/good conduct. Not all medal issues can be found online, but some information can be gleaned in this way. Waterloo medal issue can be researched at Findmypast and www.military-genealogy.com, but only if an ancestor survived until 1848. The Military Genealogy site allows you to search on name and initial for free, and displays results for Waterloo, the Boer War and the two world wars, but it is necessary to pay to view the actual records. For more advice on researching medals Peter Duckers' *British Military Medals; Guide for Collectors and Family Historians* (2009) is a useful reference book.

Information on regiments is available from regimental museums. The Army Museums Ogilby Trust has a very useful website at: www.

armymuseums.org.uk, and this features a museum search page. A search on the West Midlands region shows nine regimental museums.

Regimental Museums in the Black Country

Museum	Website
Staffordshire Regiment Museum	http://staffordshireregimentmuseum.com
Shropshire Regimental Museum	www.discovershropshire.org.uk (search under museums)
Staffordshire Yeomanry Museum	No website, tel: 01785 619131
The Queen's Own Hussars Museum	www.qohmuseum.org.uk
Royal Regiment of Fusiliers (Royal Warwickshire) Museum	www.warwickfusiliers.co.uk
Warwickshire Yeomanry Museum*	www.warwickshire-yeomanry-museum.co.uk
Worcestershire Regiment Museum Collection	www.wfrmuseum.org.uk
Worcestershire Yeomanry Museum Collection	www.worcestercitymuseums.org.uk/coll/yeoman/yeoind.htm
Herefordshire Light Infantry Museum	Email: jameshereford@waitrose.com (no website)

*Closed until spring 2013.

Each of the websites given in the table above has details of research facilities available. For the Worcestershire Regiment there are a number of documents at Worcester Record Office (see chapter 9).

Royal Air Force

The major resource for RAF records is TNA and the DocumentsOnline service at: www.nationalarchives.gov.uk/documentsonline/airforce.asp. Officer service records for the First World War and Air Ministry Combat Reports (1939–45) can be searched here. Other collections are also available, including women's RAF records and Campaign Medal Index Cards. Some officer record details are in the *Air Force List*, available at Ancestry.

During the Second World War three Black Country airports were used by the RAF: Wolverhampton, Walsall and RAF Perton, which was built in 1941 by the RAF. Alec Brew's *The History of Black Country Aviation* (1993) contains information on all three airports. See chapter 5 for details of the RAF Museums at London and Cosford.

Navy

Despite the Black Country being landlocked there will be ancestors who served in the Navy and the Royal Marines. Naval service records are not as informative as Army records, and there are no service records for ratings before 1853 as they signed on for a single voyage. TNA is the best source of information and, for example, a database of more than 18,000 individuals, all ranks, who fought at the Battle of Trafalgar can be accessed at: www.nationalarchives.gov.uk/trafalgarancestors.

After 1853 there are brief records for each rating at TNA Documents Online and you can download individual service records for a fee. TNA also provide in-depth research guides to assist you. Finally, Wikipedia have brief histories for individual ships and Bruno Pappalardo's *Tracing Your Naval Ancestors* (2003) is a useful publication.

Royal Marines

The Royal Marines are part of the Royal Navy, but have Army ranks and were an Army regiment, having formed in 1664. DocumentsOnline at TNA hold Royal Marine service records and selected Plymouth Attestations (1805–48).

Home Guard

The Home Guard operated in the Black Country and there were battalions at Tettenhall, a South Staffs Battalion (32nd South Staffs), with further battalions at Dudley, Aldridge, Stourbridge and across the Black Country. There are records at all the main archives, including photographs, notes, orders and certificates. Details of these can be found at: www.blackcountryhistory.org.

TNA is digitising 4.6 million records relating to the Home Guard. Once this is completed they will be searchable by name, date and place of birth, address and where an individual served in the Home Guard. These will hopefully be online at some point in 2012.

Appendix 2

LOCAL GOVERNMENT

Introduction

Any attempt to describe accurately and concisely the development of local government in the Black Country is beyond the scope of this volume. Two counties, a whole series of authorities, a lack of consistency across the region about when the various authorities were responsible and a growing urbanisation between the beginning of the eighteenth century and the twentieth century precludes this. This appendix describes the chronology and different forms of local government that have existed in the region. Each new type of government is detailed and, wherever possible, those towns that adopted it are listed, although these lists are not exhaustive. The current situation is that the Black Country is part of the West Midlands, yet still has its four unitary authorities of Sandwell, Dudley, Walsall and Wolverhampton.

Records of the various authorities throughout the eighteenth and nineteenth centuries have survived, but not in their entirety. Some Manorial Court Rolls are still available for consultation, and other papers can be viewed at various archives, and where they have survived their location is indicated. A simple search at www.blackcountryhistory.org will reveal a multitude of sources.

From the end of the thirteenth century Dudley was a manorial borough and from the sixteenth century to 1853 it became a Court Leet of the Lord of Dudley. Stourbridge was in the ancient Parish of Old Swinford, known as Bedcote. In 1889 it became part of Halfshire Hundred in Worcestershire. Before 1844 Halesowen was a separated part of the county of Shropshire, and in that year it was incorporated into Worcestershire. In 1958 the Local Government Act created the West Midlands Special Review Area, which included Stourbridge, Halesowen, Oldbury and Dudley.

Early Local Government – the Eighteenth Century

During the eighteenth century poor sanitary conditions, unpaved roads, rubbish collecting in the streets, poor quality water supply and over-crowding were rife across the Black Country. At the time the main instrument of local government was the manorial court. Manorial Court Rolls for Staffordshire can be found at Staffordshire Record Office, and there is a free guide on their website at: www.staffordshire.gov.uk/ Resources/Documents/m/ManorialRecordsMarch2008.pdf. Not all documents have survived, but there are plenty for Black Country towns, some dating back to the end of the eighteenth century. For Worcestershire, the Birmingham and Midland Society for Genealogy and History have documented where some records are located, and this information can be found on the Worcester branch's website at: www.worcesterbmsgh. co.uk/Halesowen.html. For Dudley there are some patchy records relating to the manors of Sedgley, Kingswinford, Oldswinford, Bedcote and Stourbridge. The other form of local government was, of course, the parish, and records covering these have been mentioned throughout the book.

Improvement Commissioners and Boards of Health

The forerunners of today's Metropolitan Borough Councils of Walsall, Wolverhampton, Sandwell and Dudley were the Improvement Commissioners and Boards of Health. Improvement Commissioners were ad hoc boards created in the eighteenth and nineteenth centuries, the first in England being the Manchester Police Commission in 1765. Commissioners had the authority to levy ratepayers and property owners for rates to pay for improvements. The powers of each board were determined by private Acts of Parliament, called Improvement Acts, and these differed for each town but were limited to areas such as street cleaning, paving, watchmen and dealing with local nuisances. Commissioners were local men of property who held votes based on the amount of property they owned or rented.

Establishment of Commissioners in Major Towns

Town	Improvement/Town Commissioners
Walsall	1824
Dudley	1791
Wolverhampton	1777
West Bromwich	1854

Boards of Health

Local Boards of Health were an important part of local government in urban areas from 1848–94. Their powers extended to controlling sewers, cleaning the streets, regulating slaughterhouses and ensuring the proper supply of water in the district. The boards were independent of the parish and had authority to take necessary action. In the 1850s and 1860s they acquired new powers and were on their way to becoming town councils. They did not replace Town or Improvement Commissioners.

Establishment of Boards of Health

Town	Board of Health
Walsall	1854
Dudley	1852

Municipal Boroughs and County Boroughs

Further reform came in 1835 with the Municipal Corporations Act which introduced a uniform system of boroughs, governed by elected town councils. Walsall became one of 178 reformed boroughs under the 1835 Act. In 1882 a further Municipal Corporations Act was passed which replaced the existing legislation. It gave corporations powers to pass byelaws and acquire land and buildings. Finally, in 1888 the Local Government Act was brought it and county councils came into being. As a result, the Black Country was divided between Staffordshire and Worcestershire as administrative counties, with Walsall, West Bromwich, Wolverhampton and Dudley as county boroughs.

Establishment of Municipal Boroughs

Town	Municipal Borough
Walsall	1835
Wolverhampton	1848
Dudley	1865
Halesowen	1936

Establishment of County Boroughs

Town	County Borough
Walsall	1835
West Bromwich	1882
Dudley	1888
Wolverhampton	1889

Urban District and Rural District Councils

The Local Government Act 1894 created urban district councils (UDC) and rural district councils (RDC) as sub-divisions of administrative counties. A UDC usually covered the area of a single parish, while a RDC could contain many parishes. UDCs were given more money than their rural counterparts because of the problems they faced by covering a larger population in a small area. Initially, there were over 1,000 UDCs, but over 200 were abolished by the Local Government Act of 1929 and some RDCs were combined with UDCs.

Establishment of Urban District Councils

Town	Urban District Council
Brierley Hill	1894 (Kingswinford RDC added 1935)
Tipton	1894
Amblecote	1898
Halesowen	1924

Brierley Hill UDC originally comprised three wards: Brierley Hill, Amblecote and Quarry Bank. Elections for councillors took place on a triennial basis and were not quite as party political as they are today, although this began to change with the rise of the Labour Party. Many early councillors tended to be local industrialists, and this was mirrored in early councils around the region. Stan Hill, a former editor of the *Blackcountryman*, became a councillor for the Thorns Ward, half of the old Quarry Bank Urban District in May 1952. His election was on the wave of the return of a Conservative government in 1951, but when the government began making cuts in spending local elections went against it. Brierley Hill UDC was a very progressive council when compared to nearby Stourbridge and, for example, in 1952 it spent £27,000 on Brierley Hill Library, whereas Stourbridge spent only £7,000 in the same period.

In 1955 a new building for civic administration was constructed in Brierley Hill, complete with an adjacent civic hall. It became surplus to requirements in 1966 when Brierley Hill UDC amalgamated with Dudley County Borough. The building remains today and is home to Brierley Hill Police Station and the civic hall continues to be used for functions. The Stafford Knot on the front of the building indicates that Brierley Hill was part of Staffordshire county at the time it was built.

During the mid-1950s the main point of debate at council meetings was about raising Brierley Hill to municipal borough status, as others, such as Tipton, Wednesbury and Rowley Regis, had all achieved this

186

status. At one stage six senior councillors refused to accept the position as chair of the UDC because they were holding off until Brierley Hill became a municipal borough so they could attempt to become the Charter Mayor. This meant that at 26 years of age Stan Hill became the youngest ever chairman of an UDC in the country.

At this time county borough boundaries were sacrosanct. In 1954 Dudley Borough were building a crematorium at Gornal Wood, Stourbridge, which at this time was in Worcestershire, but it hoped that the town would be able to use this facility. A request to Dudley Borough was turned down 'because they were in Worcestershire'. This led to Stourbridge having to build its own crematorium in South Road.

Halesowen UDC had public offices in Great Cornbow and comprised seven wards and fifteen councillors. Police stations and schools were still run by Worcestershire County Council, but councillors worked vigorously on behalf of residents to improve conditions. Halesowen Borough constructed 900 houses before the outbreak of war in 1939 and after the war estates were built at Hasbury Grange, Hasbury Farm and Fatherless Barn. They also undertook re-development in the town itself and in 1967 the precinct was opened and the Queensway built around it. Highfield Flats were completed in 1964. Halesowen's independence as a council was threatened in 1960, when there were moves for it to become part of Worcestershire County Council, but this was successfully resisted.

Establishment of Rural District Councils

Town	Rural District Council
Halesowen and Cradley	1894 (jointly)
Kingswinford (with Amblecote)	1894

Creation of the West Midlands

On 1 April 1966 five new county boroughs were created, but Halesowen and Stourbridge remained separate at this time.

Establishment of County Boroughs

Wolverhampton	Including Tettenhall, Bilston and Wednesfield
Dudley	Including Brierley Hill and Sedgley
Walsall	Including Willenhall and Darlaston
West Bromwich	Including Wednesbury and Tipton
Warley	Including Smethwick, Oldbury, Rowley Regis, Blackheath, Cradley Heath, Old Hill and Tividale

Stourbridge town hall. (Author's collection)

The final change to the local government structure came in 1974 when the West Midlands Metropolitan Borough was created. A total of four metropolitan boroughs formed the Black Country part of the wider West Midlands: Dudley, Sandwell, Walsall and Wolverhampton. The final change to the structure came in 2000 when Wolverhampton achieved city status; it is now both a city and metropolitan borough.

INDEX